SpringerBriefs in Population Studies

Advisory Editors

Baha Abu-Laban, Edmonton, AB, Canada

Mark Birkin, Leeds, UK

Dudley L. Poston Jr., Department of Sociology, Texas A&M University, College Station, TX, USA

John Stillwell, Leeds, UK

Hans-Werner Wahl, Deutsches Zentrum für Alternsforschung (DZFA), Institut für Gerontologie, Universität Heidelberg, Heidelberg, Germany

D. J. H. Deeg, VU University Medical Centre/LASA, Amsterdam, The Netherlands

SpringerBriefs in Population Studies presents concise summaries of cutting-edge research and practical applications across the field of demography and population studies. It publishes compact refereed monographs under the editorial supervision of an international Advisory Board. Volumes are compact, 50 to 125 pages, with a clear focus. The series covers a range of content from professional to academic such as: timely reports of state-of-the art analytical techniques, bridges between new research results, snapshots of hot and/or emerging topics, and in-depth case studies.

The scope of the series spans the entire field of demography and population studies, with a view to significantly advance research. The character of the series is international and multidisciplinary and includes research areas such as: population aging, fertility and family dynamics, demography, migration, population health, household structures, mortality, human geography and environment. Volumes in this series may analyze past, present and/or future trends, as well as their determinants and consequences. Both solicited and unsolicited manuscripts are considered for publication in this series.

SpringerBriefs in Population Studies will be of interest to a wide range of individuals with interests in population studies, including demographers, population geographers, sociologists, economists, political scientists, epidemiologists and health researchers as well as practitioners across the social sciences.

More information about this series at http://www.springer.com/series/10047

Guillaume Marois · Samir KC

Microsimulation Population Projections with SAS

A Reference Guide

Springer

Guillaume Marois
Asian Demographic Research Institute
Shanghai University
Shanghai, China

Wittgenstein Centre for Demography
and Global Human Capital
International Institute for Applied Systems
Analysis, University of Vienna
Laxenburg, Austria

Samir KC
Asian Demographic Research Institute
Shanghai University
Shanghai, China

Wittgenstein Centre for Demography
and Global Human Capital
International Institute for Applied Systems
Analysis, University of Vienna
Laxenburg, Austria

ISSN 2211-3215 ISSN 2211-3223 (electronic)
SpringerBriefs in Population Studies
ISBN 978-3-030-79110-0 ISBN 978-3-030-79111-7 (eBook)
https://doi.org/10.1007/978-3-030-79111-7

© The Author(s) 2021. This book is an open access publication.

Open Access This book is licensed under the terms of the Creative Commons Attribution 4.0 International License (http://creativecommons.org/licenses/by/4.0/), which permits use, sharing, adaptation, distribution and reproduction in any medium or format, as long as you give appropriate credit to the original author(s) and the source, provide a link to the Creative Commons license and indicate if changes were made.

The images or other third party material in this book are included in the book's Creative Commons license, unless indicated otherwise in a credit line to the material. If material is not included in the book's Creative Commons license and your intended use is not permitted by statutory regulation or exceeds the permitted use, you will need to obtain permission directly from the copyright holder.

The use of general descriptive names, registered names, trademarks, service marks, etc. in this publication does not imply, even in the absence of a specific statement, that such names are exempt from the relevant protective laws and regulations and therefore free for general use.

The publisher, the authors and the editors are safe to assume that the advice and information in this book are believed to be true and accurate at the date of publication. Neither the publisher nor the authors or the editors give a warranty, expressed or implied, with respect to the material contained herein or for any errors or omissions that may have been made. The publisher remains neutral with regard to jurisdictional claims in published maps and institutional affiliations.

This Springer imprint is published by the registered company Springer Nature Switzerland AG
The registered company address is: Gewerbestrasse 11, 6330 Cham, Switzerland

Contents

1 **Introduction** 1
   1.1 Why This Book? 1
   1.2 What Is Microsimulation? Why Use It? 3
   1.3 Examples of Demographic Projections Using
        Microsimulation 5
   References 7

2 **Getting Started** 11
   2.1 Properties of the Microsimulation Model 11
   2.2 The Multistate Model for India 12
   2.3 The Base Population 14
   2.4 Setting up the Workspace and Importing Parameters 21
   References 24

3 **Converting a Cohort Component Model into a Microsimulation
   Model** 25
   3.1 Mortality Event 25
   3.2 Education Module 27
   3.3 Domestic Migration Module 29
   3.4 Fertility Module 33
   3.5 Reclassification of Rural to Urban Areas 36
   3.6 Preparing the Population File for the Next Step 38
   3.7 Generating Outputs 39
   3.8 Cleaning the Workspace 43
   3.9 Simulating for Next Periods 43
   3.10 Validation of Results 46
   References 49

4 **Adding New Dimensions** 51
   4.1 Adjusting the Workspace for the Addition of New
        Dimensions 51
   4.2 Labour Force Participation Module 52
   4.3 Sector of Activity Module 58

	4.4	Including the New Dimensions in the Outputs	62
	4.5	Overview of Results	68
	References		70
5	**Building Alternative Scenarios**		**71**
	5.1	Building Alternative Scenarios from Regression Parameters	71
	5.2	Example 1: The Impact of Having a Young Child on Labour Force Participation and the Sector of Activity	72
	5.3	Example 2: Gender Equality in Labour Force Participation	74
6	**Extending and Adapting the Model**		**81**
	6.1	A Flexible Model	81
	6.2	Updating Input Files	82
	6.3	Changing the Time Span of the Projection	85
	6.4	Turning Off Modules	86
		6.4.1 Domestic Migration and Rural to Urban Reclassification	87
		6.4.2 Sector of Activity	90
	6.5	Building a Deterministic Module in a Microsimulation Model for International Migration	92
		6.5.1 Emigration	93
		6.5.2 Immigration	94
		6.5.3 Adjusting the Exposure in the Fertility Module	95
	6.6	Adjusting Outputs and the Population File for the Next Period	97
	6.7	Calibrating Simulation Outcomes	98
	6.8	Overview of Results	104
	References		106
7	**Conclusion**		**109**
	References		110

List of Figures

Fig. 1.1	Cohort component method versus microsimulation	4
Fig. 2.1	Framework of the microsimulation model	13
Fig. 2.2	Screenshot of the file aggregatedPop2010.csv (opened with Excel)	16
Fig. 2.3	Screenshot of the file POP_2010.csv (opened with Excel)	19
Fig. 3.1	Screenshot of the parameter file survival_a.csv (opened with Excel)	26
Fig. 3.2	Screenshot of the parameter file education.csv (opened with Excel)	28
Fig. 3.3	Screenshot of the origin–destination file used to create the parameter file dom_mig (opened with Excel)	30
Fig. 3.4	Screenshot of the parameter file dom_mig.csv (opened with Excel)	31
Fig. 3.5	Lexis diagram	33
Fig. 3.6	Screenshot of the parameter file ur.csv (opened with Excel)	37
Fig. 3.7	Screenshot of the results file outputpop (opened with SAS)	40
Fig. 3.8	Screenshot of the results file births (opened with SAS)	41
Fig. 3.9	Screenshot of the file output2015 (opened with SAS)	43
Fig. 3.10	Screenshot of files included in the results library (opened with SAS)	45
Fig. 3.11	Comparison of projected population size of India by educational attainment from multistate model and microsimulation, 2010–2060	48
Fig. 3.12	Comparison of the projected age pyramid in 2060 by education in India from multistate model and microsimulation	48
Fig. 3.13	Comparison of the projected population size in 2060 by region, India, from multistate model and microsimulation	49
Fig. 4.1	Predicted labour force participation rates from Eq. 4.1 by age and education, India	54
Fig. 4.2	Screenshot of the parameter file lfp.csv (opened with Excel)	55

Fig. 4.3	Arithmetic average of region-specific cohort parameters for the sector of activity converted into rate (education = complete primary; no birth in the last 5 years)	59
Fig. 4.4	Screenshot of the parameter file formal.csv (opened with Excel)	60
Fig. 4.5	Screenshot of outputpop before the transpose procedure	63
Fig. 4.6	Screenshot of outputpop after the transpose procedure	64
Fig. 4.7	Projected population by labour force status and sector of activity (left) and labour force dependency ratio (right), India, 2010–2060	69
Fig. 4.8	Projected change in the sex and education composition of the labour force, India, 2010–2060	70
Fig. 5.1	Screenshot of the parameter file lfp.csv for the YoungChild scenario (opened with Excel)	73
Fig. 5.2	Projected female labour force size in India, 2010–2060, Reference and YoungChild scenarios	73
Fig. 5.3	Projected labour force participation rate and proportion of workers in the formal sector by age in 2060, women, India, Reference and YoungChild scenarios	74
Fig. 5.4	Screenshot of the parameter file lfp.csv for the scenario GenderEquality (opened with Excel)	75
Fig. 5.5	Projected labour force participation rates by age for women, India, 2010–2060, GenderEquality scenario	78
Fig. 5.6	Projected population according to the labour force status, India, 2010–2060, Reference and GenderEquality scenarios	78
Fig. 6.1	Screenshot of the parameter file "fertility.csv" (opened with excel)	83
Fig. 6.2	Screenshot of the parameter file lfp.csv (opened with excel)	84
Fig. 6.3	Predicted labour force participation rate by age, sex and education, China. *Source* National Sample Survey on Employment and Unemployment 2017/2018 (India); Chinese General Social Survey 2010–2015 (China)	85
Fig. 6.4	Screenshot of the parameters file emig.csv (opened with excel)	94
Fig. 6.5	Screenshot of the parameter file calibration.csv (opened with excel)	101
Fig. 6.6	Comparison of the projected age pyramid in 2100 by education in China from multistate models and from microsimulation	105
Fig. 6.7	Projected total population size, working-age population (15–64) size, and labour force size, India and China, 2015–2060	106

List of Tables

Table 3.1	Error between the multistate and the microsimulation model	47
Table 4.1	Odds of working in the formal sector by level of educational attainment ($\exp(\beta_2)$ from Eq. 4.3)	59
Table 6.1	Summary of demographic assumptions for different projections	100

Chapter 1
Introduction

Abstract This chapter introduces the purpose of the book. When a researcher needs to perform microsimulation for population projections, building its own model with a common statistical software such as SAS might a good option, because this software is widely used among scholars and is taught in most social sciences departments. We define what is microsimulation: a modelling based on individual-level data rather than aggregated level data, in which transitions between the states are determined stochastically with a random experiment. We finally provide some examples of microsimulation models used by social scientists.

Keywords Microsimulation · Population projection · Demography · Method · SAS

1.1 Why This Book?

Most population projections forecast the population using only demographic characteristics (age and sex), but the inclusion of additional dimension such as education (Lutz et al. 2014) and sociocultural variables (Bélanger et al. 2019) is an emerging approach in the social sciences (Spielauer 2010). Indeed, in addition to providing a richer set of outputs, including additional dimensions provides more flexibility in the generation of policy-relevant alternative projection scenarios. Furthermore, it improves the overall quality of the projection, as more sources of heterogeneity are considered, which also allows for a more refined modeling of demographic events.

Traditional demographic projections using the cohort-component method can only provide outcomes related to the age and sex structure of a population. When extended to multistate and multiregional applications (Rogers 1980, 1995), more dimensions can also be added (such as region or education). Microsimulation is a powerful tool that can be used to create population projections when the number of dimensions becomes large. Such a model is very flexible and characterised by the stochastic simulation of individual life courses based on derived parameters and individual characteristics (Van Imhoff and Post 1998). Until the late 90s, computer power was not sufficient to use microsimulation for very complex population projection. However,

© The Author(s) 2021
G. Marois and S. KC, *Microsimulation Population Projections with SAS*,
SpringerBriefs in Population Studies,
https://doi.org/10.1007/978-3-030-79111-7_1

with a newer generation of powerful computers, some institutions around the world changed their projection methods to microsimulation (Caron-Malenfant et al. 2017).

Many microsimulation models are built using a language or a software specifically designed for this purpose, such as ModGen, JANSIM, Mic-Core, or OpenM++ (Bélanger and Sabourin 2017; Mannion et al. 2012; Zinn 2014). Using these tools requires specific and exhaustive prior knowledge, as they are complex and not user-friendly. Moreover, user guides and online support are in general limited, given the small number of users. Most of those tools are also not very flexible, as they are usually designed for a specific purpose and their functions cannot be modified or adapted easily for other purposes. This also keeps the user in the dark concerning what exactly happens when a function is called, sometimes leading to unexpected or awkward outcomes. Indeed, when using such tools, the assistance of a coding expert is generally required.

For those reasons, when a researcher needs to perform microsimulation, building one's own model with common statistical software, such as SAS, Stata, or R, might be a good option. These programs are widely used among scholars and are taught in most social science departments, so many social scientists already have the required background in the coding language. Given a large number of users, online support can also be found easily when needed.

Microsimulation packages specifically designed for population projection already exist in R (Zinn 2014). This book is a step-by-step guide showing how to build a microsimulation model for demographic projections using the SAS language. For this book, we used SAS 9.4 Codes we provide also work with other versions of SAS, such as SAS University Edition. The guide is designed for people with beginner to intermediate knowledge in SAS. We suggest codes that are easy to understand so that they can be replicated or adapted for other purposes. They are however not necessarily the most efficient.

First, this book shows how to convert an existing multistate projection by age, sex, education and region into a microsimulation model framework. Two new dimensions are then added, the labour force participation and the sector of activity, and some examples of outputs and alternative scenarios that would not be possible with standard demographic methods are shown. Other chapters show how to adapt the model for other countries or other purposes.

The book is intended for people with a good background in demography, population dynamics, and quantitative analysis, who wish to extend their technical skills by learning how to use microsimulation in demography with SAS. The user needs to know the principles of population projection, as the book does not explain how to build demographic assumptions for the future. The demographic components of the microsimulation models constructed as examples in this book come from existing multistate projections, either from KC et al. (2018) or from Lutz et al. (2018), that forecast populations by region and educational attainment. We do however build assumptions for additional dimensions of the projection, labour force participation and sector of activity, which are modelled from various surveys.

For each chapter, all input files and code files used in this book can be found in the Chapter ESM (Electronic Supplementary Materials).

1.2 What Is Microsimulation? Why Use It?

Microsimulation is an alternative approach to the deterministic macro-level population projection models that use aggregate-level data, such as the cohort-component method, to project future population dynamics. In microsimulation, the modelling is based on individual-level data. Though microsimulation methods have been conceptualised for decades and used for other purposes (Orcutt 1957), their application for population forecasts is quite new. For an exhaustive description of microsimulation for population forecasting and its properties, compared to multistate cohort-component methods, see Van Imhoff and Post (1998).

A microsimulation model starts from a baseline population that consists of individual actors whose characteristics represent the composition of a given population across chosen dimensions. These individual actors are exposed to the risk of a set of events relevant to their state and specific to their own characteristics: death, births of children (which generate new actors inside the model), moving to a different region in a country, leaving the country, achieving a level of education, entering or exiting the labour market, and so on. International immigrants enter the model with a predetermined set of individual characteristics and are subjected to risks of the events mentioned above. Transitions between the states are determined stochastically with a random experiment (Monte Carlo method). Microsimulation thus allows not only for including a larger set of dimensions than the standard multistate population projection models, in which handling more than three or four dimensions becomes challenging but also for handling competing risks easily.

Figure 1.1 shows a simple example of how stochastic microsimulation works (using the Monte Carlo method), compared to the cohort-component method. Suppose 1000 women were aged 75–79 in 2015. If we assume a probability of dying of 5%, the cohort-component method will simply remove 5% of the cohort, and we will get 950 survivals aged 80–84 in 2020.

In microsimulation, we start with a dataset in which each row is an individual. In this example, we thus have 1000 rows representing the 1000 women age 75–79 in 2015, all tagged as being alive. Some of them will die before 2020, about 5% according to our assumptions. We determine who will die with random experiments, which implies comparing the probability of dying (5%) with a linear random number between 0 and 1. When the random number is lower than the probability of dying, the individual dies, and we switch the variable alive to 0. Out of 1000, we will get about 950 survivals. When the sample is small (for instance 10 individuals), the number of survivals in a single run could be far from the expected numbers: this is the Monte Carlo error resulting from the random experiment. In these cases, it might be useful to take the average of multiple simulations or increase the sample size, which would reduce the error.

If microsimulation gives similar results to the cohort-component methods, why choose this method? Spielauer (2010) describes three broad situations when microsimulation should be used, rather than the multistate cohort-component method:

Cohort-component method

Pop$_{2015,75-79}$ $_5q_{2015,75}$ Pop$_{2020,80-84}$

1000 ➡ 5% ➡ 950

Microsimulation (Monte Carlo method)

No indiv	Alive$_{2015}$	Random		$_5q_{2015,75}$	Alive$_{2020}$
1	1	0.564	< ?	5%	1
2	1	0.391	< ?	5%	1
3	1	0.021	< ?	5%	0
4	1	0.899	< ?	5%	1
...					
1000	1	0.049	< ?	5%	0
Sum	1000				~950

Fig. 1.1 Cohort component method versus microsimulation

- When heterogeneity matters in the projection modeling or in the projection outcomes. The multistate cohort-component method can only handle a limited number of dimensions because the number of cells for the transition matrices corresponds to the multiplication of the number of categories of each dimension. In microsimulation, each additional dimension only adds a new column in the dataset. Suppose we have a 7-dimension model projecting age (20 age groups), sex (2 categories), education (6 categories), education of the mother (6 categories), region (70 categories), labour force participation (2 categories) and child parity (10 categories). The matrix for a multistate model would require more than 2 M cells (20*2*6*6*70*2*10). In microsimulation, the number of cells is the number of individuals in the sample multiplied by the number of dimensions. So if we have a sample of 100,000 individuals, the number of cells would be 700,000 (7 dimensions * 100,000). Then, if we want to add another dimension, for instance the religion in 4 categories, the number of cells in the multistate would be multiplied by 4 and would exceed 8 M, while in the microsimulation model, we just add one column to the data set and get 800,000 cells, which is much more manageable.

- *When behaviours can be better understood at the micro level than the aggregated level.* For instance, the number of years spent in a country is a major predictor for immigrants' fertility, mortality or labour force participation. At the micro level, these predictors can easily be taken into account. Only one additional column is required for the variable "time spent in the country", the value of which is incremented every year without any complex modeling. The variable can then be used in the modeling of other events, using, for instance, relative risks and logit parameters.
- *When individual histories matter.* For instance, past life habits might have a big impact on mortality and older ages. Similarly, retirement pensions depend in many cases of the past income and number of years worked. Microsimulation can also easily keep a record of the birth history of women. Every time the birth event occurs, we can just increment a variable "number of births", which can then be used once women get older to analyse their potential as caregivers.

1.3 Examples of Demographic Projections Using Microsimulation

Many types of microsimulation models have been developed and used to address different types of research questions in various fields. For example, they have been used to evaluate the future performance of long-term programs such as pensions (Morrison 2017) and long-term care (Carrière et al. 2008), to simulate the potential impacts of prospective public policies or policy changes (Sutherland 2007), and to project life-time behaviours (e.g. saving) or complex dynamics (e.g. ageing) for policy analysis (Sundberg 2007). An exhaustive overview of microsimulation applications in social sciences and other areas can be found elsewhere (Li & O'Donoghue 2013; Spielauer 2010).

Recent developments in computing technology, as well the rise in the number of micro-data sources needed to calculate the parameters of microsimulation, have made it easier to develop more complex models and have increased the level of interest in such models (Bélanger and Sabourin 2017). Those interested in reading about the different uses of specific microsimulation models and their specific methodological issues can browse the International Journal of Microsimulation,[1] which is the official peer-reviewed journal of the International Microsimulation Association.

With regard to population projections that use microsimulation, Statistics Canada, the official statistical agency of Canada, is a pioneer. The agency has used microsimulation methods for its official projections for many years. This started in 2004 with the model PopSim (now DemoSim) which was designed to project the Canadian population in terms of various characteristics (Caron-Malenfant et al. 2017). The model is built using the ModGen language and its most recent version begins with the microdata file of the National Household Survey of 2011. It projects dynamically

---

[1] https://www.microsimulation.org/ijm/.

and in continuous-time on the one hand, sociodemographic characteristics such as age, sex, education and labour force participation, and on the other hand, several ethnocultural variables, such as visible minority group, place of birth, generation status, and language.

As Canada is becoming more and more diverse with large inflows of international immigrants, the model includes explicitly the different behaviours of ethnocultural groups living in the country. Among other sources of heterogeneity, the model accounts for higher fertility for some ethnic groups (Black, Muslim, First Nations), as well as for recent immigrants, compared to those who have been living in the country longer. It accounts for the higher propensity of international immigrants to emigrate (return migration), as compared to the native population. The "healthy immigrant" effect is also implemented, which provides immigrants with lower probabilities of dying in the years following their arrival as a result of direct and indirect immigration selection (McDonald and Kennedy 2004). Domestic migration is also modulated by languages, as the French and English speakers that constitute the core of the Canadian population have very different mobility patterns.

Microsimulation is the only possible method for dynamically including such heterogeneity in sociodemographic behaviours, thus allowing for more accurate and more detailed projection outcomes. Statistics Canada has used the model to produce several reports on future Canadian populations, such as visible minority groups (Morency et al. 2017), aboriginal populations (Caron Malenfant et al. 2015), and language speakers (Houle and Corbeil 2017), and to forecast labour force participation (Martel 2019).

DemoSim is built using several confidential data files that are not available to external researchers. From public microdata files, the Laboratoire de simulations démographiques (LSD) (Demographic Simulation Laboratory) of the Institut national de la recherche scientifique (National Institute for Scientific Research) proposed a framework for a lighter version of the microsimulation model that could project the population while accounting for several sociodemographic and ethnocultural variables, in order to study population changes in a context of relatively high immigration and low fertility (Bélanger et al. 2019). This framework has been adapted to produce several region-specific versions. For instance, the LSD framework was used to build a model for the United States (Van Hook et al. 2020), LSD-USA, from the anonymised public files of the 2015 American Community Survey and General Social Surveys (1995–2015). It projects the population of the USA to 2065 and includes dimensions such as race, generation, duration of stay, education and labour force participation. LSD-USA has been used to project the effect of several policy-oriented scenarios regarding immigration levels and educational attainment on the future workforce of the country (Van Hook et al. 2020).

From the LSD framework, the Center of Expertise on Population and Migration (CEPAM), a partnership between the International Institute for Applied Systems Analysis and the Joint Research Center of the European Commission, built a similar model called CEPAM-Mic (Bélanger et al. 2019). The base population and assumptions are built from different sources: public microdata files of European Labour Force Surveys and General Social Surveys on the one hand, and aggregated data from the Census 2011 and from a multistate cohort-component model on the other hand.

The CEPAM-Mic model can dynamically project the population for the EU28 member states in terms of several socioeconomic and ethnocultural dimensions, including education, labor force participation, employment. age at immigration, region of birth, duration of residence, education of the mother, religion and language. This model allows for the study of alternative scenarios of migration and their consequences on future populations and labour supply trends in the European Union. It has been used to assess policy-relevant scenarios with regard to sociocultural inequalities in education (Marois et al. 2019a), and integration of immigrants (Marois et al. 2019b), as well as to propose an innovative dependency ratio that takes into account the productivity of workers (Marois et al. 2020). CEPAM-Mic allows researchers to assess a large range of policy-relevant alternative scenarios and produce indicators showing that population aging is less daunting than it may seem when only age structure is considered.

Beyond ethnocultural and sociodemographic variables, other types of dimensions can also be implemented in microsimulation models for demographic projections. Starting from the CEPAM-Mic model mentioned above, the model ATHLOS-Mic implements a health module that refines projection outcomes (Marois and Aktas 2021). This module adds a health metric ranging from 0 to 100 and a set of risk factors (such as smoking, obesity, etc.) to the characteristics of individuals. Changes in risk factors are determined with logit regression parameters that take into account other risk factors. The value of the health metric, which is also used to modulate the probability of dying, is then determined from risk factors and other sociodemographic characteristics. This model thus allows researchers to assess the impact of policy-intervention scenarios on different outcomes, such as the number of years of life lost or the average health of the population.

References

Bélanger, A., & Sabourin, P. (2017). *Microsimulation and population dynamics: An introduction to Modgen 12*. Springer International Publishing.

Bélanger, A., Sabourin, P., Marois, G., et al. (2019). A framework for the prospective analysis of ethno-cultural super-diversity. *Demographic Research, 41*, 293–330. https://doi.org/10.4054/DemRes.2019.41.11

Caron Malenfant, É., Coulombe, S., Langlois, S., & Morency, J.- D. (2015). Projections of the aboriginal population and households in Canada, 2011–2036. Statistics Canada, Ottawa, Canada.

Caron-Malenfant, É., Coulombe, S., & Grenier, D. (2017). Demosim: An overview of methods and data sources.

Carrière, Y., Keefe, J., & Légaré, J., et al. (2008). Projecting the future availability of the informal support network of the elderly population and assessing its impact on home care services. Statistics Canada

Houle, R., & Corbeil, J.- P. (2017). Language projections for Canada, 2011–2036. Statistics Canada, Ottawa, Canada.

Kc, S., Wurzer, M., Speringer, M., & Lutz, W. (2018). Future population and human capital in heterogeneous India. *Proceedings of the National Academy of Sciences of the United States of America, 115*, 8328. https://doi.org/10.1073/pnas.1722359115

Li, J., & O'Donoghue, C. (2013). A survey of dynamic microsimulation models: uses, model structure and methodology. *International Microsimulation Association, 6*(2), 3–55. *International Journal of Microsimulation, 6*, 3–55

Lutz, W., Butz, W. P., & KC S, (Eds.). (2014). *World Population and human capital in the twenty-first century*. Oxford, UK: Oxford University Press.

Lutz, W., Goujon, A., & KC S, , et al. (Eds.). (2018). *Demographic and human capital scenarios for the 21st century*. Luxembourg: Publications Office of the European Union.

Mannion, O., Lay-Yee, R., & Wrapson, W., et al. (2012). JAMSIM: A microsimulation modelling policy tool. *Journal of Artificial Societies and Social Simulation, 15*.

Marois, G., & Aktas, A. (2021). Projecting health-ageing trajectories in Europe using a dynamic microsimulation model. *Scientific Reports, 11*, 1785. https://doi.org/10.1038/s41598-021-81092-z

Marois, G., Sabourin, P., & Bélanger, A. (2019a). How reducing differentials in education and labor force participation could lessen workforce decline in the EU-28. *Demographic Research, 41*, 125–160.

Marois, G., Sabourin, P., & Bélanger, A. (2019b) Implementing dynamics of immigration integration in labor force participation projection in EU28. *Population Research and Policy Review*. https://doi.org/10.1007/s11113-019-09537-y

Marois, G., Bélanger, A., & Lutz, W. (2020). Population aging, migration, and productivity in Europe. *Proceedings of the National Academy of Sciences of the United States of America, 117*, 7690. https://doi.org/10.1073/pnas.1918988117

Martel, L. (2019). The labour force in Canada and its regions: Projections to 2036. Statistics Canada, Ottawa, Canada.

McDonald, J., & Kennedy, S. (2004). Insights into the "healthy immigrant effect": Health status and health service use of immigrants to Canada. *Social Science & Medicine, 59*, 1613–1627.

Morency, J.- D., Caron Malenfant, É., & MacIsaac, S. (2017) Immigration and diversity: Population projections for Canada and its regions. Statistics Canada, Ottawa, Canada.

Morrison, R. J. (2017). Rates of return in the Canada pension plan: Sub-populations of special policy interest and preliminary after-tax results. In: New frontiers in microsimulation modelling. Routledge, London.

Orcutt, G. H. (1957). A new type of socio-economic system. *The Review of Economics and Statistics, 39*, 116–123. https://doi.org/10.2307/1928528

Rogers, A. (1980). Essays in multistate mathematical demography. Laxenburg, Austria: International Institute for Applied Systems Analysis (IIASA).

Rogers, A. (1995). *Multiregional demography: Principles, methods and extensions*. Chichester, UK: Wiley.

Spielauer, M. (2010). What is social science microsimulation? *Social Science Computer Review, 29*, 9–20. https://doi.org/10.1177/0894439310370085

Sundberg, O. (2007). Model 5: SESIM (Longitudinal dynamic microsimulation model). *Modelling our future: Population ageing, health and aged care* (pp. 453–460). Bingley: Emerald Group Publishing Limited.

Sutherland, H. (2007). EUROMOD: The tax-benefit microsimulation model for the European union. *Modelling our future: Population ageing, health and aged care* (pp. 483–488). Amsterdam: Elsevier.

Van Hook, J., Bélanger, A., Sabourin, P., & Morse, A. (2020). Immigration selection and the educational composition of the US labor force. *Population and Development Review, 46*, 321–346. https://doi.org/10.1111/padr.12315

Van Imhoff, E., & Post, W. (1998). Microsimulation methods for population projection. *Population: an English Selection, 10*, 97–138.

References

Zinn, S. (2014). The MicSim package of R: An entry-level toolkit for continuous-time microsimulation. *International Journal of Microsimulation, 7*, 3–32.

Open Access This chapter is licensed under the terms of the Creative Commons Attribution 4.0 International License (http://creativecommons.org/licenses/by/4.0/), which permits use, sharing, adaptation, distribution and reproduction in any medium or format, as long as you give appropriate credit to the original author(s) and the source, provide a link to the Creative Commons license and indicate if changes were made.

The images or other third party material in this chapter are included in the chapter's Creative Commons license, unless indicated otherwise in a credit line to the material. If material is not included in the chapter's Creative Commons license and your intended use is not permitted by statutory regulation or exceeds the permitted use, you will need to obtain permission directly from the copyright holder.

Chapter 2
Getting Started

Abstract This chapter sets the stage before building the microsimulation model. First, we describe proprieties of the microsimulation model that will be built. The model is time-based, discrete-time and stochastic. We then describe properties of a multistate model that will be converted into a microsimulation model and we show how building a synthetic base population that consists of the individuals that will be projected. We finally explain how to set up the workspace in SAS.

Keywords Microsimulation · Population projection · Demography · Method · SAS

2.1 Properties of the Microsimulation Model

Various microsimulation methods exist. The one presented in this guide is as follows:

- *Time-based.* This means that we simulate the life of all individuals from time t to t + a, then repeat from t + a to t + 2 * a (in our example, from 2010 to 2015, then from 2015 to 2020, and so on until 2060). In contrast, a person-based model would simulate the life of the first individual until his death (or until the end of the projection), then simulate the life of the second one, and so on for all the individuals of the base population. The advantage of a time-based model is the possibility of using aggregated outcomes as predictors of individual events. For instance, both the size and the sociocultural composition of a municipality impact migration dynamics (Marois and Bélanger 2015). A time-based model could implement this effect.
- *Discrete-time.* This means we consider only the population at specific points in time (by 5-year steps, for instance), without considering what could happen between those points. If the projection uses 5-year steps, all probabilities of an

---

Electronic supplementary material The online version of this chapter (https://doi.org/10.1007/978-3-030-79111-7_2) contains supplementary material, which is available to authorized users.

© The Author(s) 2021
G. Marois and S. KC, *Microsimulation Population Projections with SAS*, SpringerBriefs in Population Studies,
https://doi.org/10.1007/978-3-030-79111-7_2

event need to be applied for a 5-year period. This also requires ordering the occurrence of events. For instance, we might decide that changes in education happen before fertility events. Thus, we would use the educational attainment at time t + a as a predictor of the births between t and t + a.
- *Stochastic.* All events occur stochastically using random experiments, which means we compare the probability of occurrence with a random linear number from 0 to 1 to determine whether or not the event occurs. It is also possible to perform microsimulation using a deterministic approach. This consists of multiplying the weight of individuals by the probability. We will show a quick example of this other approach later in this guide (Chap. 6).

The model described in this guide is represented schematically in Fig. 2.1 and works as follows: we start from a microdata set, which is a sample of individuals representing the starting population at time t, for instance, the population of India and its characteristics in 2010. To get the population of 2015, the dataset is then submitted to different modules that modify the characteristics of the population according to different rules and predetermined assumptions. Each module corresponds to one event (dying, giving birth, change in education, moving to a different region, etc.). Once all modules have been applied, the dataset will correspond to the population of 2015. From the resulting dataset for 2015, we then repeat the process to get the population in 2020, and so on, until the end of the projection.

The order in which modules occur matters, as they change the exposure and some events can be conditional on others. This relies in large part on the way assumptions are calculated. For instance, if migration assumptions are based on the previous place of residence as recorded in surveys or a census, then by definition, only the mobility of surviving individuals should be assessed. Therefore, in the microsimulation, the migration events should occur after the mortality event.

2.2 The Multistate Model for India

The demographic assumptions of the microsimulation model presented in Chaps. 3, 4 and 5 of this book are taken from the multistate projection by education produced by KC et al. (2018) for India and its regions. We thus replicate the demographic events (birth, mortality, migration, and change in education) from a multistate model into a microsimulation framework. More specifically, we use assumptions from the baseline scenario, taking into account differentials by education, state, and type of residence (urban/rural) for fertility and mortality. The multistate projection used as our source has the following proprieties:

- The projection time-span is from 2010 to 2100 by 5-year steps, though in our example, we project only until 2060.
- It includes 35 states of India, all classified into rural and urban areas (for a total of 70 regions).

2.2 The Multistate Model for India

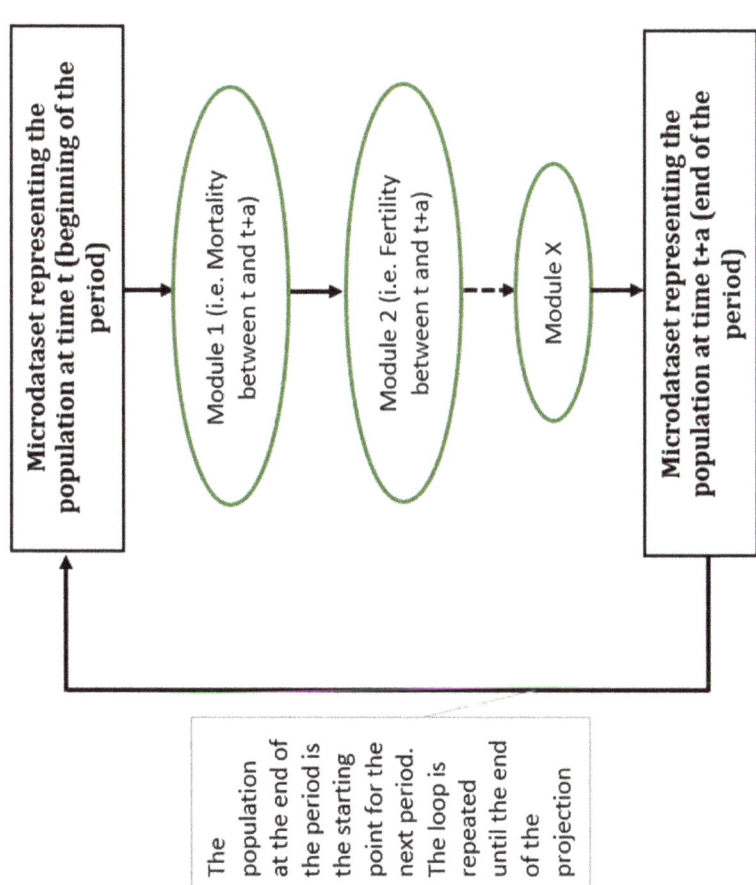

Fig. 2.1 Framework of the microsimulation model

- It includes educational attainment in 6 categories. From 0 to 14, the education variable is not applied. At the age of 15–19, the cohort is broken down according to the education level reached at this age. Transition rates are then applied and the final educational attainment is reached at the age of 30–34.
- Educational attainment matters for fertility and mortality, but not for migration.
- Before the age of 15, the education of the mother is used for mortality. However, in the base population, the education of the mother is not known, so no differentials by education are used for the populations aged 0–14 in 2010, 5–14 in 2015 and 10–14 in 2020.
- Internal mobility is modelled with an age-and sex-specific origin–destination matrix.
- In addition to internal mobility, the model allows for the reclassification of rural areas as urban areas.
- The model is closed, which means there is no international migration.

Assumptions have been formulated according to past trends, expert judgments, and statistical modeling. The detailed methodology for the assumptions is available in the supplementary information for KC et al. (2018). In this multistate projection, events are ordered as follows:

1. The mortality is applied with survival ratios by age, sex, education and region;
2. Education transition rates by age, sex, region and education are then used for educational shifts;
3. For those who survive, the domestic migration is then applied using age- and sex-specific rates from an origin–destination matrix;
4. Births are generated with fertility rates by age, education, and region applied to the exposed population;
5. Finally, region-specific reclassification rates from rural to urban areas are applied.

2.3 The Base Population

Any microsimulation model for demographic projection requires a comprehensive microdata set representing the base population. When available, the best option is to use a public microdata file of the most recent census, since it has a large sample, good coverage and good accuracy for the most relevant variables for a multidimensional population projection (age, sex, region of residence, education, etc.). Many of these files are available for free upon registration on IPUMS-International.[1] The microsimulation models for Canada and the USA developed by the *Laboratoire de Simulation Démographique* are both based on public files of recent censuses (Bélanger et al. 2019). However, variables in censuses rarely go beyond age, sex, education, and place of residence. If other variables are required in the microsimulation model, various

---

[1] https://international.ipums.org/international/.

2.3 The Base Population

imputation methods using other sources of data may be used (see for instance the MICE package in R (van Buuren and Groothuis-Oudshoorn 2011)).

When no public files of a census are available, or when they are outdated, a second option is to use a public file from a survey with a large sample (such as the *Labour Force Survey* in the European Union or *Demographic and Health Surveys* for African countries). A calibration of the microdata on aggregated data of census or population estimates may be required for optimal accuracy since surveys are not necessarily designed to be representative of the population for all variables used. This is what has been done for CEPAM-Mic, a microsimulation model projection of the population of European countries developed by the International Institute for Applied Systems Analysis (Sabourin et al. 2017). Again, variables from secondary surveys may be imputed.

Finally, when no microdata sets are available, a last option is to build one's own synthetic base population from population estimates or aggregated tables from censuses. The synthetic base population may have to follow certain rules, depending on the purpose of the projection.

For the microsimulation model showed in the example in this book, no census data files are available. The IPUMS-International provides a public file for the National Sample Survey (NSS) on Employment and Unemployment 2009, which is close to the starting year of the multistate projection (as a reminder, we want to replicate the multistate projection from KC et al. (2018) that starts in 2010), but its sample size is low for some regions, and the survey doesn't allow us to split the population by rural and urban areas. We will thus build our base population from scratch, using the aggregated population by age, sex, region, and education in 2010 from KC et al. (2018). This aggregated population can be found in the file AggregatedPop2010.csv. This input file, the complete code to generate the base population (In this Chapter—BasePop.sas) and the resulting base population (POP_2010.csv) can be found in this Chapter.

As shown in Fig. 2.2, the dataset of the input file is structured such that each line represents a possible combination of subgroups and all population counts are in one column.

Starting from this file, we build the base population in different steps. First, we import the file in SAS with proc import, which is used to import a CSV file and transform it into a SAS dataset. The datafile statement specifies the location of the CSV file (you might change this part according to your setting). The out statement specifies where we want to store the SAS dataset resulting from the importation. In our example, we store it in a file called aggregatedpop2010 located in the "work" library (the "work" library stores temporary SAS files, which means the file will be deleted after closing the session). The dbms option specifies the type of file that is imported, in our case, a CSV. The replace option indicates that an existing file will be overwritten. By giving the value "yes" to the getnames option, we finally indicate that the first row of the file is the labels of variables rather than data.

	A	B	C	D	E
1	agegr	edu	sex	region	Pop
2	0	e1	0	AN_urban	5178
3	0	e1	0	AD_urban	1084307
4	0	e1	0	AR_urban	13887
5	0	e1	0	AS_urban	160455
6	0	e1	0	BR_urban	609958
7	0	e1	0	CH_urban	41751
8	0	e1	0	CT_urban	264598
9	0	e1	0	DN_urban	8500
10	0	e1	0	DD_urban	7341
11	0	e1	0	DL_urban	713579
12	0	e1	0	GA_urban	32628
13	0	e1	0	GJ_urban	1108371
14	0	e1	0	HR_urban	413680
15	0	e1	0	HP_urban	23296
16	0	e1	0	JK_urban	162862

Fig. 2.2 Screenshot of the file aggregatedPop2010.csv (opened with Excel)

```
/*Importing the aggregated population by age, sex, education, and region*/
proc import
datafile="C:\Users\Guillaume\Desktop\Microsimulation\Chapter2\aggregatedpop2010.csv"
    out=work.aggregatedpop2010
    dbms=csv
    replace;
    getnames=yes;
run;
```

In microsimulation, we simulate individuals, so we need to disaggregate the dataset in a way that each row represents one observation. However, since the population of India is very large (more than 1 billion inhabitants), the resulting dataset of such a file would be way too large, and normal computing power is unlikely to be enough to run the simulation. We will thus apply sampling rules and weights.

The choice of the number of cases (individuals) to simulate depends on the purposes of the projection and the computer power. The larger the number of cases, the lower the Monte Carlo error. However, the computing time needed to run the simulation increases accordingly. At the national and subnational levels, a sample size higher than 500,000 cases is generally large enough to have a marginal Monte Carlo error and accurate simulation outcomes with only one single run (Bélanger et al. 2019; Caron-Malenfant et al. 2017; Marois et al. 2020; Van Hook et al. 2020). When large samples are not possible for the base population (for instance, because

2.3 The Base Population

of limited computing power or because the base population is built from a survey), multiple runs of the microsimulation may be required (Van Imhoff and Post 1998). In this book, since the base population we build is synthetic, we can decide a priori the number of cases to simulate. Therefore, we choose a number that will be large enough to produce accurate national and subnational outcomes with a single microsimulation run. If we want to analyse a more disaggregated group further (for instance, women with a high level of education in a specific region), we can either increase the sample size for the group of interest or perform multiple runs of the simulation.

The first thing to do is to remove from the dataset the groups with 0 population (such as the children with a high level of education), which reduces the size of the dataset. We create a new temporary dataset called pop from the imported dataset aggregatedpop2010. When the variable pop (for population size) is 0, we delete the row.

```
/*Removing categories with 0 population*/
data work.pop;
set work.aggregatedpop2010;
if pop=0 then delete;
run;
```

For large enough population counts, for example, larger than 10,000, individuals can be used to represent a percentage of the population. We decided in our example that the number of simulated individuals would represent 0.05% of the population size. Using a do loop, the principle of the code to do so is to replicate rows that meet this condition (10,000 ≤pop, that is, when the population is higher than 10,000). The number of replications corresponds to the multiplication of the population size by 0.0005 (0.05%) minus 1 (the initial row of the replication is already there).

```
/*Generating individuals for the base population*/
data work.pop;
set work.pop;

if 10000<=pop then do i=1 to (pop*0.0005-1);
weight=pop/(pop*0.0005)+(pop-floor(pop*0.0005)*pop/(pop*0.0005))/floor(pop*0.0005);
output;
end;
output;

run;
```

In the replication process, a weight variable is created at the same time. Since we set the sample size to 0.05%, the weight of each replication is about 2000 (pop/(pop*0.0005)). However, because the population size is in general not a perfect fraction of 0.0005, we need to adjust the weight. The "do loop" only uses integers, so when the population size is for instance 13,800, there are 5 loops and the sum of weights of those 6 observations (the 5 replications plus the initial observation) is 12,000. The difference between 13,800 and 12,000 divided by the number of observations (that we get using the floor, which rounds down a value) is added to the weight of each observation.

For groups with smaller populations, using the same sample rule might generate too few observations, which would lead to less accurate forecasting results by increasing the Monte Carlo error. At the same time, the dataset would be too loaded if we included too many observations for groups that are very marginal (such as women 90–95 with a postsecondary education living in a rural area of Dadra & Nagar Haveli). We, therefore, decided to generate a specific number of observations that decreases with the population size of the group: 40 observations for populations between 1000 and 10,000, 30 observations for populations between 100 and 1000, 10 for populations between 30 and 100 and 2 for populations lower than 30.

To alleviate the codes, we create a macro function that will repeat the codes to generate individuals under different parameters for the thresholds in population size and the number of observations to generate. The macro function starts with %macro followed by the name of the macro and the parameters in bracket. The code to repeat is then stated, while parameters are preceded by the symbol &. For our purpose, the name of the macro is "sample". The parameters are minpop (for the minimum population threshold), maxpop (for the maximum population threshold) and size (for the number of individuals to generate). The code embedded in the function is then the one shown above in the example for populations larger than 10,000, adding however an upper limit to the condition (&maxpop) and replacing 10,000 with &minpop and "pop*0.0005" with &size.

```
/*Generating individuals for the base population*/
%macro sample(minpop, maxpop, size);
data work.pop;
set work.pop;
if &minpop<=pop<&maxpop then do i=1 to (&size-1);
weight=pop/(&size)+(pop-floor(&size)*pop/(&size))/floor(&size);
output;
end;
output;
run;
%mend;
```

We can then call the macro with different parameters to generate the desired number of observations in the dataset.

```
%sample(0,30,2);
%sample(30,100,10);
%sample(100,1000,30);
%sample(1000,10000,40);
```

If not generated already, we can also use the macro for populations larger than 10,000.

```
%sample(10000,100000000,(pop*0.0005));
```

The resulting dataset now has 846,024 observations with an average population weight of 1431.2 (maximum 2398.2) and a standard variation of 890.5. Now that the dataset is disaggregated, we can prepare the dataset for the microsimulation in the new temporary dataset pop2010. We add a variable year with the value 2010, which is the starting year of the projection we replicate. This variable will be updated further in the microsimulation. From the age group variable, we create the cohort of birth. We add a variable for the education of the mother. This variable will only be used as a determinant of the mortality of children. For those already born in 2010, there are no differentials, so the value doesn't matter in the base population. By default, all the individuals in the base population are alive, so we set the variable death = 0. This will

2.3 The Base Population

change further during the simulation. Finally, we drop variables pop and i that were used to generate the observations, as they will not be used in the microsimulation.

```
/*Preparing the dataset for the microsimulation*/
data work.pop2010;
set work.pop;

    /*Starting year*/
    year=2010;

    /*Cohort*/
    cohort=year-5-agegr;

    /*Education of the mother, set the same as own education temporarily*/
    eduM=edu;

    /*All individuals are alive*/
    death=0;

drop pop i;
run;
```

The last step in the creation of the base population is to export the dataset in a CSV file. We use the export procedure. In the outfile statement, we specify the location and name of the exported file (POP_2010.csv). With dbms, we specify the type of file (CSV). Finally, the replace option overwrites any existing file with the same name.

```
/*Exporting the base population in a csv file*/
proc export data=work.pop2010
outfile=C:\Users\Guillaume\Desktop\Microsimulation\Chapter\POP_2010.csv'
dbms=csv replace;
run;
```

The resulting CSV file has 9 columns (Fig. 2.3). The complete base population can be downloaded online.

The values of variables are as follows:

agegr—Age group of.
  0. 0-4;
  5. 5-9;
  10. 10–14;
  …

	A	B	C	D	E	F	G	H	I
1	agegr	edu	sex	region	weight	year	cohort	eduM	death
2	0	e1	0	AN_urban	129.4587	2010	2005	e1	0
3	0	e1	0	AN_urban	129.4587	2010	2005	e1	0
4	0	e1	0	AN_urban	129.4587	2010	2005	e1	0
5	0	e1	0	AN_urban	129.4587	2010	2005	e1	0
6	0	e1	0	AN_urban	129.4587	2010	2005	e1	0
7	0	e1	0	AN_urban	129.4587	2010	2005	e1	0
8	0	e1	0	AN_urban	129.4587	2010	2005	e1	0

Fig. 2.3 Screenshot of the file POP_2010.csv (opened with Excel)

100. 100+;

edu—Educational attainment/*eduM*—Education of the mother.
   e1. No education;
   e2. Incomplete primary;
   e3. Complete primary;
   e4. Lower secondary;
   e5. Upper secondary;
   e6. Postsecondary;

sex—Sex.
   0. Male;
   1. Female;

region—Region of residence.
   (followed by *_rural* for rural parts and *_urban* for urban parts)
   AD. Andhra Pradesh;
   AN. Andaman & Nicobar Islands;
   AR. Arunachal Pradesh;
   AS. Assam;
   BR. Bihar;
   CH. Chandigarh;
   CT. Chhattisgarh;
   DD. Daman & Diu;
   DL. Nct Of Delhi;
   DN. Dadra & Nagar Haveli;
   GA. Goa;
   GJ. Gujarat;
   HP. Himachal Pradesh;
   HR. Haryana;
   JH. Jharkhand;
   JK. Jammu & Kashmir;
   KA. Karnataka;
   KL. Kerala;
   LD. Lakshadweep;
   MH. Maharashtra;
   ML. Meghalaya;
   MN. Manipur;
   MP. Madhya Pradesh;
   MZ. Mizoram;
   NL. Nagaland;
   OR. Odisha;
   PB. Punjab;
   PY. Puducherry;
   RJ. Rajasthan;
   SK. Sikkim;

TN. Tamil Nadu;
TR. Tripura;
UP. Uttar Pradesh;
UT. Uttarakhand;
WB. West Bengal;

weight—Sample weight (individual).

year—Year of observation.

cohort—Year of birth.
   1905. 1905-1909;
   1910. 1910-1914;
   …
   2005. 2005-2009;

death–Death status.
   0. Alive;
   1. Death;

2.4 Setting up the Workspace and Importing Parameters

In Chaps. 3 and 4, we will project the population for India and its regions from 2010 to 2060. In the support documents provided with this book (Chapter ESM), the folders for Chaps. 3 to 6 are divided into three subfolders. The subfolder "Population" includes the disaggregated population file of the projection year by year. Before running the simulation, the only file is the base population in CSV generated in the previous step of this chapter (BasePop_2010.csv). The subfolder "Parameters" contains the parameter files in CSV (fertility rates, survival ratios, etc.) that will be used for the projection. Finally, the subfolder "Outputs", empty before running the simulation, will contain the projection aggregated outcomes (population counts and components of growth).

Starting from the base population of 2010 we described above, we want to generate the projection population in 2015, then 2020, and so on until 2060. Every step follows exactly the same equations, though with different parameters. Thus, we only need to do the coding for one step, such as from 2010 to 2015 in the example that follows. Further, we will translate the code into a macro function that repeats the process for every step until 2060.

Before coding the microsimulation model, we need to set up the workspace. The complete code for this purpose can be found in this Chapter—BasePop.sas and is also replicated in the code of the complete microsimulation provided for other chapters.

First, using the %let statement, we define the name of the scenario in a variable stored as "scenario_name". Further in the code, we can then use "&scenario_name" at every place where the name of the scenario has to be recalled. This allows us to simplify the creation of alternative scenarios, as the name of the scenario would just need to be changed once (with the %let statement). In our example, the name of the scenario will first be Chap. 3. This will be changed in other chapters.

```
%let scenario_name=Chapter3;
```

Second, we define libraries, each of which is a collection of files located in a single folder.[2] Here, we define three libraries. The first one, called "pop", is the folder where the population files are (including the base population). The "param" library is the one where the parameters files are located (e.g. fertility rates, mortality rates, regression parameters, etc.). Finally, the "results" library is the folder where projection outcomes are stored. All of these folders are subfolders of the folder "Chap. 3" which is recalled using &scenario_name. The datasets procedure is used to erase results from a previous preliminary run of the projection (if you didn't run anything yet, this statement won't do anything).

```
libname pop "C:\Users\Guillaume\Desktop\Microsimulation\%scenario_name\population ";
libname param "C:\Users\Guillaume\Desktop\Microsimulation\%scenario_name\parameters";
libname results "C:\Users\Guillaume\Desktop\Microsimulation\%scenario_name\outputs";
proc datasets lib=results kill nolist memtype=data; quit;
```

Third, we import the CSV files that will be required and convert them into SAS files (.sas7bbat). Here, rather than repeating the code to import every file, we create a macro "import" (using %macro < code > %mend;) and call it with %import. The macro parameter "source" stands for the path of the CSV file, while the parameter "destination" is the name and location of the converted file. For instance, in the first call of the macro, we import the CSV file of the base population (base_pop2010.csv) and convert it into a SAS file stored in the library pop. The other imported files are the parameters for the events:

- survival_a.csv are survival ratios (sx) for adults (15+) are.
- survival_k.csv are survival ratios (sx) for kids (less than 15 yo). Kids and adults are split into two files, because predictors are different (the education is used for adults, while the education of the mother is used for kids).
- fertility.csv are fertility rates.
- srb.csv are the sex ratios at birth.
- education.csv are the transition rates for the progression of education.
- dom_mig.csv are the mobility rates between regions.
- ur.csv are the reclassification rates of rural to urban area.
- lfp.csv are logit regression parameters for the modeling of the labour force participation (used in Chap. 4).
- formal.csv are logit regression parameters for the modeling of the sector of activity (used in Chap. 4).
- lfp_imput.csv are logit regression parameters for the imputation of the labour force participation in the base population (used in Chap. 4).

---

[2] If you use SAS University Edition, the folder needs to be in the shared folder specified when configuring the server. For the standard SAS, the folder can be located anywhere.

2.4 Setting up the Workspace and Importing Parameters

- formal_imput.csv are logit regression parameters for the imputation of the sector of activity in the base population (used in Chap. 4).

```sas
/*Importing parameters and data*/
%MACRO import(source,destination);
PROC IMPORT OUT=&destination
            DATAFILE=&source
            DBMS=csv REPLACE;
       GETNAMES=YES;
       guessingrows=1000;
RUN;
%MEND;

%import
("C:\Users\Guillaume\Desktop\Microsimulation\%scenario_name\parameters
\Population\POP_2010.csv ",pop.pop_2010);
%import
("C:\Users\Guillaume\Desktop\Microsimulation\%scenario_name\parameters
\parameters\survival_a.csv",param.survival_a);
%import
("C:\Users\Guillaume\Desktop\Microsimulation\%scenario_name\parameters
\parameters\survival_k.csv",param.survival_k);
%import
("C:\Users\Guillaume\Desktop\Microsimulation\%scenario_name\parameters
\parameters\fertility.csv",param.fertility);
%import
("C:\Users\Guillaume\Desktop\Microsimulation\%scenario_name\parameters
\parameters\srb.csv",param.srb);
%import
("C:\Users\Guillaume\Desktop\Microsimulation\%scenario_name\parameters
\parameters\education.csv",param.education);
%import
("C:\Users\Guillaume\Desktop\Microsimulation\%scenario_name\parameters
\parameters\dom_mig.csv",param.dom_mig);
%import
("C:\Users\Guillaume\Desktop\Microsimulation\%scenario_name\parameters
\parameters\ur.csv",param.ur);
%import
("C:\Users\Guillaume\Desktop\Microsimulation\%scenario_name\parameters
\parameters\lfp.csv",param.lfp);
%import
("C:\Users\Guillaume\Desktop\Microsimulation\%scenario_name\parameters
\parameters\formal.csv",param.formal);
%import
("C:\Users\Guillaume\Desktop\Microsimulation\%scenario_name\parameters
\parameters\lfp_imput.csv",param.lfp_imput);
%import
("C:\Users\Guillaume\Desktop\Microsimulation\%scenario_name\parameters
\parameters\formal_imput.csv",param.formal_imput);
```

The structure of each of these files will be explained in the section of the corresponding event. At this step, we also sort the imported files (the proc sort statement). When datasets are merged (which will be done later), they need to be sorted by the same variables.

```sas
proc sort data=param.survival_a; by region agegr edu sex year;run;
proc sort data=param.survival_k; by region agegr eduM sex year;run;
proc sort data=param.fertility; by region agegr edu sex year;run;
proc sort data=param.education; by region agegr sex year;run;
proc sort data=param.dom_mig; by region agegr edu sex;run;
proc sort data=param.ur; by region;run;
proc sort data=param.srb; by region year;run;
```

References

Marois, G., & Bélanger, A. (2015). Analyzing the impact of urban planning on population distribution in the Montreal metropolitan area using a small-area microsimulation projection model. *Population and Environment, 37*, 131–156. https://doi.org/10.1007/s11111-015-0234-7

Kc, S., Wurzer, M., Speringer, M., & Lutz, W. (2018). Future population and human capital in heterogeneous India. *Proceedings of the National Academy of Sciences of the United States of America, 115*, 8328. https://doi.org/10.1073/pnas.1722359115

Bélanger, A., Sabourin, P., Marois, G., et al. (2019). A framework for the prospective analysis of ethno-cultural super-diversity. *Demographic Research, 41*, 293–330. https://doi.org/10.4054/DemRes.2019.41.11

van Buuren, S., & Groothuis-Oudshoorn, K. (2011). mice: Multivariate imputation by chained equations in R. *Journal of Statistical Software, 1*(3), 2011.

Sabourin, P., Marois, G., & Bélanger, A. (2017). The base population of the CEPAM microsimulation model.

Caron-Malenfant, É., Coulombe, S., & Grenier, D. (2017). Demosim: An overview of methods and data sources.

Marois, G., Bélanger, A., & Lutz, W. (2020). Population aging, migration, and productivity in Europe. *Proceedings of the National Academy of Sciences of the United States of America, 117*, 7690. https://doi.org/10.1073/pnas.1918988117

Van Hook, J., Bélanger, A., Sabourin, P., & Morse, A. (2020). Immigration selection and the educational composition of the US labor force. *Population and Development Review, 46*, 321–346. https://doi.org/10.1111/padr.12315

Van Imhoff, E., & Post, W. (1998). Microsimulation methods for population projection. *Population, 10*, 97–138.

Open Access This chapter is licensed under the terms of the Creative Commons Attribution 4.0 International License (http://creativecommons.org/licenses/by/4.0/), which permits use, sharing, adaptation, distribution and reproduction in any medium or format, as long as you give appropriate credit to the original author(s) and the source, provide a link to the Creative Commons license and indicate if changes were made.

The images or other third party material in this chapter are included in the chapter's Creative Commons license, unless indicated otherwise in a credit line to the material. If material is not included in the chapter's Creative Commons license and your intended use is not permitted by statutory regulation or exceeds the permitted use, you will need to obtain permission directly from the copyright holder.

Chapter 3
Converting a Cohort Component Model into a Microsimulation Model

Abstract In this chapter, we show and explain the code that reproduces the multistate projection of India described in Chap. 2 into a microsimulation model. The microsimulation code is divided into modules for each demographic event, namely the mortality, the education, the fertility, the domestic migration, and the reclassification of rural to urban areas. Section by section, we explain the code for the simulation and the production of outputs. We also a basic validation of the mode. The code file "Chapter 3—Replicating multistate.sas" contains the final complete code that generates the simulation for 2010–2060, including the setting up of the workspace (see Chap. 2).

Keywords Microsimulation · Population projection · Demography · Method · SAS

3.1 Mortality Event

The parameter files for the mortality module are survival_a (for adults' mortality) and survival_k (for children's mortality). As a reminder, parameters for adults and children are split into two files because they don't have the same predictors. However, both files have the same structure. In this example, survival ratios (sx_a or sx_k) by year, age, sex, region and education (for adults)/education of the mother (for kids) are used for the modeling of mortality. Files are structured such that all parameters are in one single column, and each line corresponds to one possible combination of education category, age group, sex and region, as shown below in the image of the first lines of the dataset survival_a. The value 0.990324 for sx_a represents the probability of surviving the next 5 years (up to 2015) for a male (sex = 0) in the age group 15–19 (agegr = 15) with no education (edu = e1) living in a rural area of

---

Electronic supplementary material The online version of this chapter (https://doi.org/10.1007/978-3-030-79111-7_3) contains supplementary material, which is available to authorized users.

	A	B	C	D	E	F
1	year	sex	agegr	edu	region	sx_a
2	2010	0	15	e1	AD_rural	0.990324
3	2010	0	20	e1	AD_rural	0.987227
4	2010	0	25	e1	AD_rural	0.984276
5	2010	0	30	e1	AD_rural	0.979242
6	2010	0	35	e1	AD_rural	0.972255
7	2010	0	40	e1	AD_rural	0.961296
8	2010	0	45	e1	AD_rural	0.945148
9	2010	0	50	e1	AD_rural	0.922248
10	2010	0	55	e1	AD_rural	0.885773

Fig. 3.1 Screenshot of the parameter file survival_a.csv (opened with Excel)

Andhra Pradesh (region = AD_rural) in 2010. Note that in the dataset survival_k, the agegr = -5 corresponds to the survival ratios for children that will be born during the period. Those will be used in the fertility module (Fig. 3.1).

We need to allocate to all individuals of the base population of 2010 their corresponding survival ratio. To do so, we first merge the parameters file survival_a to the population of 2010 in a temporary dataset (pop_survival1) located in the temporary library "work". We specify variables to take into account in the merging with the "by" statement, in this case: region, agegr, edu, sex and year. The option "in = in1" followed by "if in1" is used to keep only observations from the population file (in other words, if there is no match in the population file for a specific survival ratio, the line will be deleted).

```
/*Mortality module*/
    /*For children age<15, we use the education of the mother.
     Therefore, we pick parameters in a different dataset*/
    data work.pop_survival1;
    merge pop.pop_2010(in=in1) param.survival_a;
    by region agegr edu sex year;
    if in1;
    run;
```

Similarly, after sorting pop_survival1, we then create a second temporary dataset, pop_survival2, in which we add survival ratios for kids (using eduM—the education of the mother—in the merge statement rather than edu). In the base population, we do not know what the education of the mother. Thus, for those cohorts aged 0–14 in 2010, no differentials by mother's education are implemented. Those differentials will only be applied for new cohorts generated throughout the projection.

3.1 Mortality Event

```
proc sort data= work.pop_survival1; by region agegr eduM sex year;run;
    data work.pop_survival2;
    merge work.pop_survival1(in=in1)  param.survival_k;
    by region agegr eduM sex year;
    if in1;
    (…)
```

Depending on the age of the individual (below or above 15), we attribute the appropriate sx (either from survival_a, which are sx_a, or from survival_k, which are sx_k).

```
(…)
if agegr<=15 then sx=sx_k;
if agegr>15 then sx=sx_a;
(…)
```

Now that each individual has their own survival ratio, the temporary dataset is ready to simulate the mortality event with a random experiment. For this, we compare sx to a random number (from 0 to 1) following a uniform distribution generated with "rand('uniform')". If sx is lower than the random number, then the individual will die during the period (death $= 1$). At this point, we don't yet delete him from the dataset, because we still need to consider him in the exposed population of other events that will be modelled in further steps such as fertility.

```
(…)
if rand('uniform')>sx then death=1;
(…)
```

Once we know who will survive and who will die during the period, we can then remove the survival ratios with the *drop* statement, since they will not be used anymore (different sx will be used for further periods).

```
drop sx sx_a sx_k;
run;
```

3.2 Education Module

The education variable has 6 categories. Transitions in education may only occur in one direction (from a lower level to the next upper level) and only at certain ages. Children below the age of 15 are classified in a specific category in the outputs. The education variable thus starts at the age of 15. Before that age, the education of the mother is used in events such as mortality. The parameters for the education module are stored in the file education.csv, the structure of which is shown in Fig. 3.2.

Transitions vary by sex, age, region, and year. There are two types of parameters, and they start with the prefixes "e" and "pe", respectively. Parameters starting with "e" are only applied to the population age 10–14 at time t and correspond to educational attainment at age 15–19 (time t + 5). For instance, among males (sex $= 0$) who were age 10 (agegr $= 10$) in 2010 and living in a rural part of Andhra Pradesh (region $=$ AD_rural), 13.9% will have a complete primary education (e3) as a higher level

	A	B	C	D	E	F	G	H	I	J	K	L
1	sex	agegr	year	region	e2	e3	e4	e5	e6	pe4	pe5	pe6
2	0	10	2010	AD_rural	0.019676	0.139038	0.17938	0.575099	0.018768	0	0	0
3	0	15	2010	AD_rural	0	0	0	0	0	0	0.343771	0.361183
4	0	20	2010	AD_rural	0	0	0	0	0	0.012108	0.023131	0.085319
5	0	25	2010	AD_rural	0	0	0	0	0	0.018848	0.048247	0.010175
6	0	10	2015	AD_rural	0.014472	0.143229	0.185251	0.594921	0.019408	0	0	0
7	0	15	2015	AD_rural	0	0	0	0	0	0	0.473058	0.376329
8	0	20	2015	AD_rural	0	0	0	0	0	0.008798	0.072366	0.09179
9	0	25	2015	AD_rural	0	0	0	0	0	0.015036	0.031584	0.007449
10	0	10	2020	AD_rural	0.010552	0.145952	0.189266	0.608558	0.019853	0	0	0
11	0	15	2020	AD_rural	0	0	0	0	0	0.143779	0.584226	0.389758
12	0	20	2020	AD_rural	0	0	0	0	0	0.00583	0.158749	0.101361
13	0	25	2020	AD_rural	0	0	0	0	0	0.011746	0.023993	0.006875
14	0	10	2025	AD_rural	0.007655	0.147451	0.191666	0.617543	0.020136	0	0	0
15	0	15	2025	AD_rural	0	0	0	0	0	0.285765	0.678805	0.401433
16	0	20	2025	AD_rural	0	0	0	0	0	0.003337	0.239352	0.110323
17	0	25	2025	AD_rural	0	0	0	0	0	0.008562	0.015157	0.005805

Fig. 3.2 Screenshot of the parameter file education.csv (opened with Excel)

of education at age 15–19 in 2015. The category e1 is omitted in parameters, as it corresponds to 1 minus the sum e2 to e6.

The second type (pe) of parameter is the probabilities of change from level e3 to e4 (pe4), from e4 to e5 (pe5) and from e5 to e6 (pe6) between t and t + 5. These parameters are applied from the age group 15–19 to 25–29 at time t (so 20–24 to 30–34 at time t + 5). In our example, a man in the age group 15–19 living in a rural part of Andhra Pradesh and having an upper secondary education in 2010 has a 36.1183% chance of completing postsecondary education by 2015.

There are no transitions between other education categories, such as between incomplete primary (e2) and complete primary (e3), as at the age of 15–19, most of those individuals who do not have at least a complete primary education (e3) are already out of the education system, and their current educational attainment is the one they will have for the rest of their life.

The first step in the code of the education module is the merging of the parameter file (education) to the last population file resulting from the mortality module (work.pop_suvival2) by the relevant variables (in our example, region, agegr, sex and year) into a new temporary population file (pop_edu) in which the education event will occur.

```
/*Education module*/
    proc sort data=work.pop_survival2; by region agegr sex year;run;
    data work.pop_edu;
    merge work.pop_survival2(in=in1) param.education;
    by region agegr sex year;
    if in1;
    (…)
```

We then generate a linear random variable that we store in the temporary variable "a", and we create another temporary variable "edu_new" for which the initial value is the same as the current level of education (edu). We then simulate changes in education. First, by comparing the random variable "a" to parameters e2 to e6, we assign the educational attainment at the age 15–19 at time t + 5 (so to the population

3.2 Education Module

in the age group 10–14 at time t). Since the education variable has many categories, we need to use cumulative probabilities in order to have only one alternative for each value of "a". The default value of new_edu is "e1", so if the random variable "a" is higher than the cumulative proportions of "e2" to "e6", the category "e1" is kept.

```
(...)
a=rand('uniform');
edu_new=edu;
if agegr=10 then do;
    if a<e2 then edu_new='e2';
    if e2<=a<(e2+e3) then edu_new='e3';
    if (e2+e3)<=a<(e2+e3+e4) then edu_new='e4';
    if (e2+e3+e4)<=a<(e2+e3+e4+e5) then edu_new='e5';
    if (e2+e3+e4+e5)<=a<(e2+e3+e4+e5+e6) then edu_new='e6';
end;
(...)
```

For the population age 15–19 to 25–29, we then simulate transitions from the category "e3" to "e4", from "e4" to "e5" and from "e5" to "e6" using parameters "pe4", "pe5" and "pe6" respectively, that we compare with the random variable "a".

```
(...)
if 15<=agegr<=25 then do;
    if edu in ('e3') and a<pe4 then edu_new='e4';
    if edu in ('e4') and a<pe5 then edu_new='e5';
    if edu in ('e5') and a<pe6 then edu_new='e6';
end;
(...)
```

The projection uses fertility rates by education as an input. To have good exposure for those rates, we create a variable "edu_fert" that is for half of the population the education at the beginning of the period (at this point, it is still the variable edu) and for the other half, the education at the end of the period (the variable edu_new).

```
edu_fert=edu;
if rand('uniform')<0.5 then edu_fert=edu_new;
```

Finally, we replace the value of edu with the value of edu_new. The variable edu is now the education level that will be reached at t + 5. We drop parameters ("e2-e6", "pe5" and "pe6") and temporary variables ("a" and "edu_new").

```
(...)
edu=edu_new;
drop a edu_new e2-e6 pe4-pe6;
run;
```

3.3 Domestic Migration Module

Interregional (or domestic) migration can be modelled in different ways. In our example, we use rates in an origin–destination (O–D) matrix. For other dimensions we have modelled up to now, the number of states was small and few transitions were possible. For the mortality module, there are only two states and only one transition is possible, from alive to dead. In the education module, there are 6 states and transitions are only possible in one direction (from a lower level to the next upper level). In the case of domestic mobility, we have in this example 70 regions and it is possible for an individual to move to any of them in any stage of life.

The original parameters from the multistate projection are an OD matrix in which each possible combination of age, sex, education, region of origin and region of destination has its own rate (Fig. 3.3). The probability of a male (sex = 0) between 30 and 34 years of age (agegr = 30) with no education (edu = e1) living in an urban area of Andaman & Nicobar Islands (region = AN_urban) will move to an urban area of Andhra Pradesh (AD_urban) is thus 0.7042%. Values in the diagonal are very high, as they represent the probability of staying in the origin region (89.6198% in this example). The matrix includes the education dimension, but in the reference scenario no differentials have been implemented. This dimension might however be used in a further extension of the assumptions.

In the case of a multistate event such as this one, we need to rearrange the file in order to have cumulative probabilities for the different alternatives, as shown in Fig. 3.4. Otherwise, if we use the same type of structure as used for the mortality module, a random number might be lower than more than one destination region. For the case presented above, the cumulative probability corresponding to the mobility from AN_urban to AD_urban would thus be 90.324%, either the probability of staying in AN_urban (89.6198%) + the probability of moving to AD_urban (0.7042%). For all cases, the value of the last option would thus be 1. Once structured in this way, only one region will correspond to a random number between 0 and 1.

	A	B	C	D	E	F	G	H	I	J	K	L	M
1	sex	agegr	edu	region	AN_urban	AD_urban	AR_urban	AS_urban	BR_urban	CH_urban	CT_urban	DN_urban	DD_urban
2	0	30	e1	AN_urban	0.896198	0.007042	0.000041	0.000285	0.000102	0.000265	0.000020	0.000020	0.000000
3	0	30	e1	AD_urban	0.000034	0.974024	0.000002	0.000025	0.000018	0.000031	0.000163	0.000009	0.000004
4	0	30	e1	AR_urban	0.000014	0.000153	0.944825	0.002429	0.000201	0.000076	0.000035	0.000000	0.000000
5	0	30	e1	AS_urban	0.000006	0.000219	0.000945	0.972931	0.000280	0.000178	0.000076	0.000005	0.000005
6	0	30	e1	BR_urban	0.000011	0.000493	0.000059	0.000373	0.956394	0.000140	0.000583	0.000064	0.000015
7	0	30	e1	CH_urban	0.000017	0.000239	0.000004	0.000067	0.000137	0.941175	0.000096	0.000015	0.000022
8	0	30	e1	CT_urban	0.000001	0.000183	0.000003	0.000015	0.000074	0.000052	0.972335	0.000004	0.000002
9	0	30	e1	DN_urban	0	0.000211	0.000000	0.000106	0.000106	0.000053	0.000106	0.961594	0.002009
10	0	30	e1	DD_urban	0.000116	0.000232	0.000039	0.000000	0.000425	0.000039	0.000077	0.001391	0.952345
11	0	30	e1	DL_urban	0.000019	0.000451	0.000007	0.000050	0.000114	0.000491	0.000073	0.000008	0.000006
12	0	30	e1	GA_urban	0.000251	0.001261	0.000006	0.000017	0.000026	0.000037	0.000023	0.000006	0.000167
13	0	30	e1	GJ_urban	0.000003	0.000201	0.000001	0.000017	0.000038	0.000038	0.000037	0.000061	0.000066
14	0	30	e1	HR_urban	0.000005	0.000181	0.000007	0.000075	0.000084	0.001341	0.000137	0.000009	0.000005
15	0	30	e1	HP_urban	0.000015	0.000328	0.000065	0.000198	0.000148	0.005537	0.000136	0.000025	0.000012
16	0	30	e1	JK_urban	0.000007	0.000283	0.000017	0.000099	0.000146	0.000509	0.000081	0.000007	0.000001
17	0	30	e1	JH_urban	0.000006	0.000149	0.000005	0.000038	0.002004	0.000060	0.000767	0.000011	0.000003
18	0	30	e1	KA_urban	0.000007	0.000936	0.000002	0.000012	0.000012	0.000041	0.000019	0.000010	0.000007
19	0	30	e1	KL_urban	0.000079	0.001018	0.000024	0.000043	0.000022	0.000045	0.000084	0.000027	0.000023
20	0	30	e1	LD_urban	0.000094	0.000377	0.000000	0.000000	0.000189	0.000000	0.000094	0.000094	0.000094
21	0	30	e1	MP_urban	0.000001	0.000204	0.000002	0.000017	0.000031	0.000040	0.001760	0.000011	0.000004
22	0	30	e1	MH_urban	0.000014	0.000521	0.000001	0.000014	0.000023	0.000039	0.000151	0.000063	0.000032
23	0	30	e1	MN_urban	0	0.000120	0.000171	0.000585	0.000060	0.000687	0.000029	0.000003	0.000000
24	0	30	e1	ML_urban	0.000028	0.000220	0.000312	0.002852	0.000101	0.000202	0.000046	0.000005	0.000000
25	0	30	e1	MZ_urban	0.000007	0.000029	0.000083	0.000237	0.000050	0.000058	0.000004	0.000000	0.000000
26	0	30	e1	NL_urban	0	0.000096	0.000191	0.001907	0.001109	0.000100	0.000048	0.000000	0.000000
27	0	30	e1	OR_urban	0.000014	0.001187	0.000008	0.000056	0.000140	0.000036	0.000972	0.000025	0.000015
28	0	30	e1	PY_urban	0.000002	0.000332	0.000002	0.000012	0.000040	0.000025	0.000017	0.000010	0.000000

Fig. 3.3 Screenshot of the origin–destination file used to create the parameter file dom_mig (opened with Excel)

3.3 Domestic Migration Module

	A	B	C	D	E	F	G	H	I	J	K	L	M
1	sex	agegr	edu	region	AN_urban	AD_urban	AR_urban	AS_urban	BR_urban	CH_urban	CT_urban	DN_urban	DD_urban
2	0	30	e1	AN_urban	0.896198	0.90324	0.903281	0.903566	0.903668	0.903933	0.903953	0.903973	0.903973
3	0	30	e1	AD_urban	0.000034	0.974058	0.97406	0.974085	0.974103	0.974134	0.974297	0.974306	0.97431
4	0	30	e1	AR_urban	0.000014	0.000167	0.944992	0.947421	0.947622	0.947698	0.947733	0.947733	0.947733
5	0	30	e1	AS_urban	0.000006	0.000225	0.00117	0.974101	0.974381	0.974559	0.974635	0.97464	0.974645
6	0	30	e1	BR_urban	0.000011	0.000504	0.000563	0.000936	0.95733	0.95747	0.958053	0.958117	0.958132
7	0	30	e1	CH_urban	0.000017	0.000256	0.00026	0.000327	0.000464	0.941639	0.941735	0.94175	0.941772
8	0	30	e1	CT_urban	0.000001	0.000184	0.000187	0.000202	0.000276	0.000328	0.972663	0.972667	0.972669
9	0	30	e1	DN_urban	0	0.000211	0.000211	0.000317	0.000423	0.000476	0.000582	0.962176	0.964185
10	0	30	e1	DD_urban	0.000116	0.000348	0.000387	0.000387	0.000812	0.000851	0.000928	0.002319	0.954664
11	0	30	e1	DL_urban	0.000019	0.00047	0.000477	0.000527	0.000641	0.001132	0.001205	0.001213	0.001219
12	0	30	e1	GA_urban	0.000251	0.001512	0.001518	0.001535	0.001561	0.001598	0.001621	0.001627	0.001794
13	0	30	e1	GJ_urban	0.000003	0.000204	0.000205	0.000222	0.00026	0.000298	0.000335	0.000396	0.000462
14	0	30	e1	HR_urban	0.000005	0.000186	0.000193	0.000268	0.000352	0.001693	0.00183	0.001839	0.001844
15	0	30	e1	HP_urban	0.000015	0.000343	0.000408	0.000606	0.000754	0.006291	0.006427	0.006452	0.006464
16	0	30	e1	JK_urban	0.000007	0.00029	0.000307	0.000406	0.000552	0.001061	0.001142	0.001149	0.00115
17	0	30	e1	JH_urban	0.000006	0.000155	0.00016	0.000198	0.002202	0.002262	0.003029	0.00304	0.003043
18	0	30	e1	KA_urban	0.000007	0.000943	0.000945	0.000957	0.000969	0.00101	0.001029	0.001039	0.001046
19	0	30	e1	KL_urban	0.000079	0.001097	0.001121	0.001164	0.001186	0.001231	0.001315	0.001342	0.001365
20	0	30	e1	LD_urban	0.000094	0.000471	0.000471	0.000471	0.00066	0.00066	0.000754	0.000848	0.000942
21	0	30	e1	MP_urban	0.000001	0.000205	0.000207	0.000224	0.000255	0.000295	0.002055	0.002066	0.00207
22	0	30	e1	MH_urban	0.000014	0.000535	0.000536	0.00055	0.000573	0.000612	0.000763	0.000826	0.000858
23	0	30	e1	MN_urban	0	0.00012	0.000291	0.000876	0.000936	0.001623	0.001652	0.001655	0.001655
24	0	30	e1	ML_urban	0.000028	0.000248	0.00056	0.003412	0.003513	0.003715	0.003761	0.003766	0.003766
25	0	30	e1	MZ_urban	0.000007	0.000036	0.000119	0.000356	0.000406	0.000464	0.000468	0.000468	0.000468
26	0	30	e1	NL_urban	0	0.000096	0.000287	0.002194	0.003303	0.003403	0.003451	0.003451	0.003451
27	0	30	e1	OR_urban	0.000014	0.001201	0.001209	0.001265	0.001405	0.001441	0.002413	0.002438	0.002453
28	0	30	e1	PY_urban	0.00002	0.000352	0.000354	0.000366	0.000406	0.000431	0.000448	0.000458	0.000458

Fig. 3.4 Screenshot of the parameter file dom_mig.csv (opened with Excel)

For the code, in a new population file (pop_dm), we merge the parameter file (dom_mig) to the last population file (pop_edu). Each individual will therefore have a (cumulative) probability of staying in the origin region and a (cumulative) probability of moving to any other region.

```
/*Domestic migration module*/
proc sort data= work.pop_edu; by region agegr edu sex year; run;
data work.pop_dm;
merge work.pop_edu (in=in1) param.dom_mig;
by region agegr edu sex;
if in1;
(...)
```

We store the origin region in a new variable "oldregion", which will be used in subsequent steps. We generate a random number that we store in a temporary variable "a". The random number needs to be tracked because the same number needs to be used in different places in modeling the event. We then create an array called *prob* that states the regions ({*}is used to specify that the number of elements in the array is the number of arguments that follows).

```
(...)
oldregion=region;
a=rand('uniform');
array prob{*}AN_urban AD_urban  AR_urban  AS_urban  BR_urban  CH_urban  CT_urban
DN_urban   DD_urban   DL_urban  GA_urban  GJ_urban  HR_urban  HP_urban  JK_urban
JH_urban   KA_urban   KL_urban  LD_urban  MP_urban  MH_urban  MN_urban  ML_urban
MZ_urban   NL_urban   OR_urban  PY_urban  PB_urban  RJ_urban  SK_urban  TN_urban
TR_urban   UT_urban   UP_urban  WB_urban  AN_rural  AD_rural  AR_rural  AS_rural
BR_rural   CH_rural   CT_rural  DN_rural  DD_rural  DL_rural  GA_rural  GJ_rural
HR_rural   HP_rural   JK_rural  JH_rural  KA_rural  KL_rural  LD_rural  MP_rural
MH_rural   MN_rural   ML_rural  MZ_rural  NL_rural  OR_rural  PY_rural  PB_rural
RJ_rural   SK_rural   TN_rural  TR_rural  UT_rural  UP_rural  WB_rural;
(...)
```

Using the *do* statement on all elements stated in the array *prob*, we compare the random number "a" to the cumulative probability for every destination region i. When "a" is lower than the cumulative probability of region i, but higher than the one for the previous region ($i-1$), the label of the corresponding element in the array (we select it with the *vname* statement) is then assigned to the temporary variable "newregion". For the first region in the array ($i = 1$, AN_urban in our example), we just compare the cumulative probability to the random number a ($i-1$ doesn't exist). Thus, for any random number generated, only one option is possible.

```
(...)
do i=1 to dim(prob);
    if i=1 and a<prob(i) then newregion=vname(prob[i]);
    if 1<i and prob(i-1)<=a<prob(i) then newregion=vname(prob[i]);
end;
(...)
```

Once done, the variable "region" corresponds to the region of residence at time *t*, while the variable newregion corresponds to the region at time $t + 5$. As we did for the education module, we need to create a special variable in order to have the proper exposed population in the fertility module. We can assume that half of the migrants are exposed to the fertility rate of the destination, while the other half are exposed to the origin's fertility rates. Therefore, we create accordingly a variable "region_fert" that will be used for the region of exposure in the fertility module.

```
(...)
region_fert=region;
if rand('uniform')<0.5 then region_fert=newregion;
(...)
```

When variables region and newregion are the same, the individual did not move. In order to count the number of migrants, we create a variable "dom_mig" that takes the value of 1 when "newregion" and "region" are different. We then replace the value of the variable "region" with the new region. The number of emigrants by region can therefore be obtained by doing a crosstable of dom_mig and oldregion, while the number of immigrants can be obtained by doing a crosstable of "dom_mig" and "region". Note that in our example, only the population that survives until $t + 5$ (death $= 0$) can migrate, because data to estimate the mobility come from the question on the previous residence in censuses, which by definition is asked to the surviving population only.

```
(...)
if death=0 and newregion ne region then do; dom_mig=1; region=newregion; end;
(...)
```

3.3 Domestic Migration Module

Finally, we drop the temporary variables (i a newregion) and variables for parameters (AN_urban–WB_rural), because they will not be used anymore.

```
(...)
drop i a AN_urban--WB_rural newregion;
run;
```

In our example, rates are constant throughout the projection. To make them evolve, we can simply add a column "year" to the dom_mig file, filling in the rates for the future, and adding "year" as in merging variables.

3.4 Fertility Module

The fertility module is a bit more complex since when the event happens, a new individual (having its own characteristics) must be generated and added to the population file. Also, it needs to take into account that this new individual might not survive between birth and time $t + a$.

Over a 5-year-period, a cohort age X at time t will also be exposed to the risk of fertility of age group X and X + 5. The Lexis diagram below (Fig. 3.5) shows an example of exposure between t and $t + 5$ for the cohort age 15–19 at time t (the red lozenge). The cohort has half of the risk in the age group 15–19 (in orange), half of the risk in 20–24 (in light blue). The rates for the age group 20–24 (green square) is thus applied to two cohorts.

Fig. 3.5 Lexis diagram

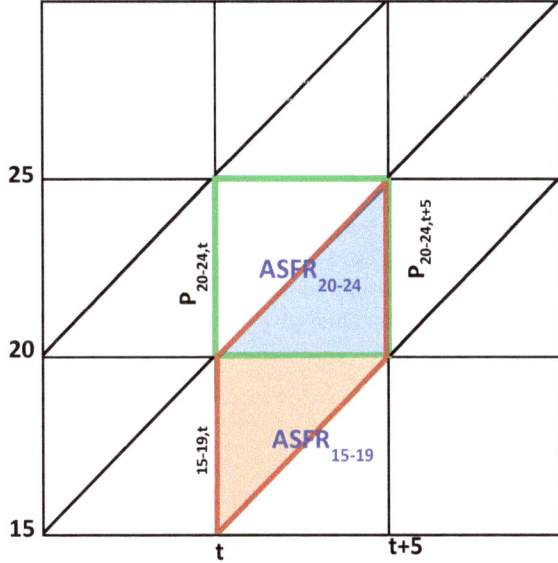

To expose the population to appropriate fertility rates, in a new temporary population file (pop_birth) created from the last population file (pop_dm), we create a new variable "agegr_fert" that corresponds to the variable used for the age at fertility. We assume half of the population will change age group before the middle of the period. Therefore, agegr_fert is the same as the age group for half of the population, while for the other half, it corresponds the age group + 5. The split is done randomly by comparing a random number distributed uniformly between 0 and 1 generated with rand ('uniform') to 0.5.

```
/*Fertility module*/
    /*Adjusting age for exposure*/
    data work.pop_birth;
    set work.pop_dm;
    agegr_fert=agegr;
    if rand('uniform')<0.5 then agegr_fert=agegr+5;
    run;
(...)
```

Similar exposure-adjusted variables have been created for the education and the region of residence in their respective modules. After sorting the population file properly, in a new population (pop_birth1), we then implement the fertility rates from the parameter file param.fertility. Note that the link variables used are specific to the fertility module: agegr_fert, region_fert and edu_fert. Then, in a similar way, in a new population file pop_birth2, we add the parameters file for the sex ratio at birth by region and year (param.srb).

```
/*Implementing parameters*/
proc sort data=work.pop_birth; by region_fert agegr_fert edu_fert sex year;run;
data work.pop_birth1; merge work.pop_birth(in=in1) param.fertility; by region_fert agegr_fert edu_fert sex year; if in1; run;
proc sort data=work.pop_birth1; by region_fert year;run;
data work.pop_birth2;
merge work.pop_birth1(in=in1) param.srb ;
by region_fert year;
if in1;
(...)
```

We can then proceed to the fertility event. First, we reset the variable identifying the mother of a young kid, since children born during the previous period will change age group. The events are applied to surviving individuals (death = 0) and to half of the deaths that we select randomly, as we assume that they die on average in the middle of the period. Then, using the Monte Carlo method, we simulate the fertility event: when a random uniform variable between 0 and 1 is lower than the fertility rate, then the individual gives birth during the period (identified with the variable young_kid).

```
/*Fertility event*/
young_kid=0;
    if death=0 or (death=1 and rand('uniform')<0.5) then do;
        if rand('uniform')<5*asfr then young_kid=1;*Has a kid age 0-4;
    end;
(...)
```

3.4 Fertility Module

Once a woman gives birth, we generate a new individual to add to the population: her baby. For this purpose, we use the output statement,[1] which duplicates the line of the mother. We then have to determine the characteristics of the baby. A flag variable birth is first created (birth = 1), in order to compile the number of births in a further step. We also create a variable stating the age of the mother that can further be used in outputs. We assign the age group "−5" to the baby (as a reminder, −5 stands for those who are born between t and $t + 5$, while 0 is for those aged 0–4 at time t). We also define the year of birth in the variable "cohort" (2010 would thus stand for babies born between 2010 and 2014).

Then, with another random experiment, we determine if the baby is a boy or a girl using the sex ratio at birth (SRB) parameter (the variable srb—sex ratio at birth, which comes from the file srb.csv). The srb is expressed in this case as the number of baby girls for 1000 baby boys. Although in most countries, this is usually always about the same (about 953 girls for 1000 boys), it's much lower in India because of sex-selective abortions that are very common in some regions (Retherford and Roy 2003). Thus, the SRB has region- and year-specific values, allowing us to build assumptions for its future evolution.

(...)
```
/*Create newborn and set their characteristics*/
output;
if young_kid=1 then do;
    birth=1;
    age_moth=agegr_fert;
    agegr=-5; young_kid=0; death=0; cohort=year; region_birth=region_fert;
    dom_mig=0; if region_birth ne region then dom_mig=1;
    sex=0; if rand('uniform')<(srb/(srb+1000)) then sex=1;
    eduM=edu_fert;
    edu='e1';
    if 5*asfr>1 then weight=weight*5*asfr;
    output;
end;
run;
```

Since the line for the baby is a duplication of the line of the mother, the sample weight of the mother is automatically transferred to the baby. The region is also transferred, but, as a reminder, since the domestic mobility module occurs before, it now corresponds to the region at the end of the period and not the region at birth. The region at birth is the variable used for the exposure to fertility, region_fert, that we store in another variable, "region_birth", which will be used when generating the outputs of the components of growth. When this region of birth differs from the region of residence at the end of the period, the baby is flagged as a domestic migrant (dom_mig = 1).

We also keep track of the education of the mother in the variable eduM (which is used for the mortality until the age of 15), and set the education of the baby to e1 (no education).

The projection uses 5-year steps, so it is possible to have a fertility rate higher than 1 for a specific group. In such cases, the rate will always be higher than the

---

[1] See the SAS documentation for more details about the output statement: https://documentation.sas.com/?docsetId=lestmtsref&docsetTarget=n1lltvbis7ye1an1eryo4leh2mck.htm&docsetVersion=9.4&locale=en.

random number generated for the fertility event, and some births will be missing. On average, more than one birth occurs per woman, so a simple way to get the correct number of births is to adjust the population weight of the baby by multiplying it by the fertility rate (such as what would be done in a deterministic microsimulation; see Chap. 6). In the case of a woman with a weight of 1000 and a fertility rate of 1.2, the weight of the newborn would thus be 1200.

The last step of the fertility module is to simulate the survival of the baby between the birth and the end of the period ($t + 5$). For this purpose, we will again need to use the parameters file containing survival ratios for kids (survival_k). We merge it with our last population file (pop_birth2), by region, age, sex, education of the mother and year. We then simulate the mortality event for babies born between t and $t + 5$ (identified by agegr $= -5$), the same way we did in the mortality module for the living population at time t. Because the mortality event occurs before migration, the region at death is the one where the baby is born (region $=$ region_birth). Finally, since we don't need them anymore, we drop temporary variables and parameters.

```
/*Simulate the survival of babies*/
proc sort data=work.pop_birth2; by region agegr eduM sex year; run;
data work.pop_birth3;
merge work.pop_birth2(in=in1) param.survival_k;
by region agegr eduM sex year; if in1;

if agegr=-5 then do;
    if rand('uniform')>sx_k then do; death=1; region=region_birth; end;
        end;
drop sx_k asfr srb agegr_fert edu_fert region_fert;
run;
```

3.5 Reclassification of Rural to Urban Areas

With the rapid urbanisation of India, cities are spreading and absorbing some rural areas. Thus, some people's environments can switch from rural to urban without migration. The multistate model provides annual rates of the reclassification of rural areas by region, age, sex and education. Those rates are included in the parameters file "urbanisation", in the column "ur", as illustrated in Fig. 3.6. Rates are region-specific and constant throughout the projection. The number 0.040471 for the region AD_rural mean that about 4% of the population living in a rural area of Andhra Pradesh are reclassified as living in an urban area every 5 years. We can note that some rates are very high, such as the one for Dadra & Nagar Havel (DN_rural) which is almost 67%. Regions with such high rates have small areas and rapid urbanisation. Consequently, the rural areas in such regions are expected to disappear within the next few decades.

The reclassification event occurs after all other demographic events. After sorting the last population file (pop_birth3) by region, we merge it with the parameters file that includes the reclassification rates (param.ur) in a new temporary population file

3.5 Reclassification of Rural to Urban Areas

Fig. 3.6 Screenshot of the parameter file ur.csv (opened with Excel)

	A	B
1	region	ur
2	AD_rural	0.040471
3	AN_rural	0.033443
4	AR_rural	0.009291
5	AS_rural	0.019746
6	BR_rural	0.004528
7	CH_rural	0.508552
8	CT_rural	0.003557
9	DD_rural	0.214488
10	DL_rural	0.569817
11	DN_rural	0.667174
12	GA_rural	0.235545
13	GJ_rural	0.021988
14	HP_rural	0.028253
15	HR_rural	0.003228
16	JH_rural	0.022537
17	JK_rural	0.033185
18	KA_rural	0.017052
19	KL_rural	0.289824
20	LD_rural	0.585807
21	MH_rural	0.006803
22	ML_rural	0.02518
23	MN_rural	0.064766
24	MP_rural	0.020649
25	MZ_rural	0
26	NL_rural	0.034304
27	OR_rural	0.016038
28	PB_rural	0.070555
29	PY_rural	0.024741
30	RJ_rural	0.01492
31	SK_rural	0.021413
32	TN_rural	0.047827
33	TR_rural	0.084389
34	UP_rural	0.030316
35	UT_rural	0.010827
36	WB_rural	0.066503

called pop_reclass. Each individual living in a rural area now has a probability of being reclassified as living in an urban area.

For the coding of the event, we first store the old region in another variable (oldregion2). This variable will be used later when generating outputs of the projection. The event only applies to those who are still alive at this point of the projection (death = 0) and those living in a rural area, which we can select using the substr function. Options in the brackets of this function mean that we look to see if the 5 characters starting from the 4th character of the variable "region" contain the string "rural".

```
/*Reclassification of rural to urban areas*/
proc sort data=work.pop_birth3; by region; run;
data work.pop_reclass;
merge work.pop_ birth3 (in=in1) param.ur;
by region;
if in1;

oldregion2=region;
if death=0 and substr(region,4,5)='rural' then do;
    if rand('uniform')<ur then do;
    region=tranwrd(region,'rural','urban');
    reclass=1; end;
end;

drop ur;
run;
```

Once the appropriate population is selected, the event is modelled with the Monte Carlo method, comparing a random number to the reclassification rate (ur). When the event happens, the function transwrd is used to change the value of the region variable from rural to urban. The first term in the brackets of this function selects the variable to modify (region); the second term identifies the string of characters to replace ('rural'); and the third term is the string of characters of substitution ('urban'). We keep track of reclassified individuals in a new variable labelled "reclass", which will be used when generating outputs. Finally, we drop the reclassification rates (ur) from the dataset, as they won't be used anymore.

3.6 Preparing the Population File for the Next Step

We have simulated changes in the population characteristics for the first 5 years of the projection. All demographic events are completed. We now have to prepare the population file for the next step. First, we make our population ages and we increment the year in a small "time module". Starting from our last population file (pop_reclass), we create a new one (pop2) in which the year is increased by 5 as well as the age of survival (death = 0). For those who died during t and $t + 5$ (except for babies born during the period), we assume that only half died before their anniversary. This last statement will only be useful for outputs related to the age distribution of diseases.

3.6 Preparing the Population File for the Next Step

```
/*Time module - Updating characteristics*/
data work.pop2;
set work.pop_reclass;
if death=0 or agegr=-5 then agegr=agegr+5;
if death=1 and agegr ne -5 and rand('uniform')<0.5 then agegr=agegr+5;
year=year+5;
run;
```

The population file pop2 represents the population at the end of the period, but still includes the deaths, which are flagged with the variable death = 1. For the next period of the projection, those individuals need to be removed. From pop2, we create a new population file "pop_2015" that is the surviving population in 2015. This file is stored in the library pop because it is the final projected population for 2015. We delete the deaths from the dataset and we drop variables that were used as flags for births, migrants, and individuals who were reclassified from rural to urban areas.

```
/*Cleaning the population file for next period*/
data pop.pop_2015;
set work.pop2;

if death=1 then delete;
drop birth dom_mig reclass oldregion oldregion2 region_birth;
run;
```

3.7 Generating Outputs

The population file pop_2015 is the dataset corresponding to the surviving population in 2015. The file pop_reclass is the last file containing a record of demographic events (with variables birth, death, dom_mig and reclass). From these two files, we will generate projection outputs. Variables included in this step of the model may vary according to the needs of the user. The code for generating outputs has no impact on the projection.

First, from the population file pop_2015, we create a flat file outputpop that aggregates the population by sex, region, age group and education. The option noprint is used, because the output is stored in a separate dataset (out=) and we don't need to display the table in SAS. The option list is used to create one single table in which each column corresponds to a variable and each row is a specific combination of categories. The options norow, nocol, nopercent and nocum are stated in order to keep only frequencies in the table and to remove percentages and sums. In the output file, the column "count" is renamed "pop", as it represents the population size.

```
/*Generating outputs*/
    /*Population per age sex region and education*/
    proc freq data=pop.pop_2015 noprint;
    table  year*agegr*sex*edu*region /list norow nocol nopercent nocum
out=work.outputpop (rename=(count=pop) drop=percent);
    weight weight;
    run;
```

An excerpt of the resulting file is shown in Fig. 3.7. Remember that since

3 Converting a Cohort Component Model into a Microsimulation Model

	YEAR	agegr	SEX	edu	region	Frequency Count
1	2015	0	0	e1	AD_rural	2065319.0371
2	2015	0	0	e1	AD_urban	1316830.3415
3	2015	0	0	e1	AN_rural	9347.477045
4	2015	0	0	e1	AN_urban	4516.1015791
5	2015	0	0	e1	AR_rural	46320.596953
6	2015	0	0	e1	AR_urban	15613.463698
7	2015	0	0	e1	AS_rural	1449413.2988
8	2015	0	0	e1	AS_urban	242234.76644
9	2015	0	0	e1	BR_rural	5845179.0957
10	2015	0	0	e1	BR_urban	618466.87054
11	2015	0	0	e1	CH_rural	103.71906272
12	2015	0	0	e1	CH_urban	44317.066877
13	2015	0	0	e1	CT_rural	1205542.2086
14	2015	0	0	e1	CT_urban	267268.05909
15	2015	0	0	e1	DD_rural	4677.4048404
16	2015	0	0	e1	DD_urban	8288.0561332
17	2015	0	0	e1	DL_rural	11171.145541
18	2015	0	0	e1	DL_urban	679071.59736

Fig. 3.7 Screenshot of the results file outputpop (opened with SAS)

microsimulation is based on a stochastic process using random experiments, results may differ slightly on each run.

In our example, we also want to generate outputs for components of the growth. We need to use the temporary file pop2 for that purpose, since it is the last one that keeps track of demographic events, including births, deaths, domestic migration (both inflows and outflows), and individuals reclassified from rural to urban areas. We use the FREQ procedure to create frequency tables for each component.

For the birth event, we select births (birth = 1) with the *where* statement. In the *table* statement, we split births by age of the mother, education of the mother, sex, and region of birth, and in options, we specify that we want to keep only frequencies. We also rename the variable education of the mother (eduM = edu), the age of the mother (age_moth = age) and the region of birth (region_birth = region), because we will later merge this file with the population count. The resulting table is stored in the dataset *births* in the temporary library *work*. An excerpt of the table is shown in Fig. 3.8.

```
/*Components of population growth*/
proc freq data=work.pop_reclass noprint;
  table year*age_moth*eduM*region_birth/list norow nocol nopercent nocum
out=work.birth(rename=(count=births age_moth=agegr eduM=edu region_birth=region)
drop=percent);
  weight weight;
  where birth=1;
run;
```

3.7 Generating Outputs

	year	agegr	edu	region	Frequency Count	sex
1	2015	15	e1	AD_rural	256329.93481	1
2	2015	15	e1	AD_urban	60235.141728	1
3	2015	15	e1	AN_rural	335.49081605	1
4	2015	15	e1	AN_urban	196.16959913	1
5	2015	15	e1	AR_rural	7472.0108875	1
6	2015	15	e1	AR_urban	3643.6293627	1
7	2015	15	e1	AS_rural	417782.12225	1
8	2015	15	e1	AS_urban	29036.251312	1
9	2015	15	e1	BR_rural	804778.52632	1
10	2015	15	e1	BR_urban	72230.703591	1
11	2015	15	e1	CH_rural	147.14945392	1
12	2015	15	e1	CH_urban	978.53899438	1
13	2015	15	e1	CT_rural	144660.53704	1

Fig. 3.8 Screenshot of the results file births (opened with SAS)

Using flag variables identifying deaths, migrants and reclassified individuals, we generate similar frequency tables for deaths, inflows, outflows, and changes from rural to urban areas, though we replace the education and age of the mother with the education and age of the individual (and remove the rename statement accordingly). For outflows and individuals reclassified from rural to urban areas, we need to state the former region of residence (oldregion and oldregion2, respectively) rather than the current one, and rename the variable in the dataset in order to allow us to merge it with another dataset later. For reclassified individuals, we also need to exclude domestic migrants (dom_mig ne 1) from the tables in order to avoid double counts. For both rural to urban reclassification and domestic migration, because they are implemented after the mortality event, we also add death = 0 in order to avoid counting a baby that died between the birth and the end of the year (the rest of the deceased population was already excluded in the modeling of the event).

```sas
    proc freq data=work.pop2 noprint;
    table year*agegr*sex*edu*region/list norow nocol nopercent nocum
out=work.death(rename=(count=deaths) drop=percent);
    weight weight;
    where death=1;
    run;

    proc freq data=work.pop2 noprint;
    table year*agegr*sex*edu*region/list norow nocol nopercent nocum
out=work.inflow(rename=(count=inflow) drop=percent);
    weight weight;
    where dom_mig=1 and death=0;
    run;

    proc freq data=work.pop2 noprint;
    table year*agegr*sex*edu*oldregion/list norow nocol nopercent nocum
out=work.outflow(rename=(count=outflow oldregion=region) drop=percent);
    weight weight;
    where dom_mig=1 and death=0;
    run;

    proc freq data=work.pop2 noprint;
    table year*agegr*sex*edu*region/list norow nocol nopercent nocum
out=work.gain_urban(rename=(count=gain_urban) drop=percent);
    weight weight;
    where reclass=1 and dom_mig ne 1 and death=0;
    run;

    proc freq data=work.pop2 noprint;
    table year*agegr*sex*edu*oldregion2/list norow nocol nopercent nocum
out=work.loss_rural(rename=(count=loss_rural oldregion2=region) drop=percent);
    weight weight;
    where reclass=1 and dom_mig ne 1 and death=0;
    run;
```

We now have 7 datasets of outputs, one for the population count and six for components of growth. We will now merge them into a single dataset. We first need to add a column "sex", taking the value of 1 for everyone in the file birth2015, because we want births to match the female population only.

```sas
/*Merging the population count and components of growth*/
data work.birth2015;
set work.birth2015;
sex=1;
run;
```

We can now merge all those files in a new dataset called "output2015" stored in the "results" library. Using an array called "change" that included numeric variables (selected with _numeric_), we switch missing values to 0 and remove decimals using the *round* statement.

```sas
    data results.output2015;
    merge work.outputpop work.birth work.death work.inflow work.outflow work.gain_urban
work.loss_rural;
    by year agegr sex edu region;

    array change _numeric_;
      do over change;
        if change=. then change=0;
        change=round(change);
      end;
    run;
```

As shown in Fig. 3.9, the resulting file output2015 now includes the population size by age, education, sex and region, as well as the components of growth for every specific sub-group.

3.8 Cleaning the Workspace

	year	agegr	sex	edu	region	pop	births	deaths	inflow	outflow	gain_urban	loss_rural
1	2015	0	0	e1	AD_rural	2296885	0	104380	31277	36721	0	111923
2	2015	0	0	e1	AD_urban	1283619	0	18110	32821	32317	111923	0
3	2015	0	0	e1	AN_rural	8767	0	0	176	122	0	533
4	2015	0	0	e1	AN_urban	7106	0	0	2018	314	533	0
5	2015	0	0	e1	AR_rural	43621	0	217	484	173	0	65
6	2015	0	0	e1	AR_urban	15826	0	0	2180	736	65	0
7	2015	0	0	e1	AS_rural	1614077	0	82165	4264	12050	0	34701
8	2015	0	0	e1	AS_urban	197020	0	6107	10291	4051	34701	0
9	2015	0	0	e1	BR_rural	5815113	0	218505	32260	75622	0	23028
10	2015	0	0	e1	BR_urban	649526	0	14909	34233	23513	23028	0
11	2015	0	0	e1	CH_rural	548	0	6	0	205	0	4632
12	2015	0	0	e1	CH_urban	47528	0	0	8498	1178	4632	0
13	2015	0	0	e1	CT_rural	1158028	0	59435	13047	23423	0	2028
14	2015	0	0	e1	CT_urban	302290	0	8137	20510	19348	2028	0
15	2015	0	0	e1	DD_rural	2406	0	72	29	55	0	3204
16	2015	0	0	e1	DD_urban	10237	0	15	59	184	3204	0
17	2015	0	0	e1	DL_rural	17178	0	11	6116	638	0	11653
18	2015	0	0	e1	DL_urban	799251	0	6042	77001	16056	11653	0

Fig. 3.9 Screenshot of the file output2015 (opened with SAS)

3.8 Cleaning the Workspace

During the simulation of events, we created many temporary datasets. Before passing to the next period, we need to remove them from the memory. The code below is used to clean all datasets stored in the *work* library.

```
/*Clean temporary dataset*/
proc datasets lib=work kill nolist memtype=data;
quit;
```

3.9 Simulating for Next Periods

Up to now, we simulated the population for one step, from time t to $t + 5$ (2010 to 2015 in our example). We started from a base population file (pop_2010), and we ended up with another population file having the same structure for 2015 (pop_2015). This file is now the starting point for the next step, from 2015 to 2020. We could just use the same code, but call it pop_2015 rather than pop_2010 in the first module (mortality), changing the name of the final population file in the module preparing the population file for the next step (pop_2020 rather than pop_2015) and changing the years in the name of the outcome files.

Doing this, though easy, would however require many lines of code. For this kind of situation where codes are repeated with only small changes, SAS allows the user to create a macro that stores the repetitive code in a function and in which elements to change are identified as parameters. To run the code, we can further call the macro function and specify the appropriate parameters.

To create a macro, we need to insert the repeating code between statements *%macro name* and *%mend name*. Parameters are declared in brackets after stating the name of the macro, and would refer to the code identified by the same label with the prefix & in the codes.

In our example, we will create a macro called *micosim* with parameters *styr* (for starting year) and *endyr* (for ending year). The code to repeat starts by sorting the initial population file. We thus declare the macro just before this code with *%macro microsim(styr,endyr)*. Then, throughout the codes, we change labels that refer to the starting year (2010) by *&styr* and those that refer to the ending year (2015) by *&endyr*. We highlight them in yellow in the code below.

```
%macro microsim(styr,endyr);

proc sort data=pop.pop_&styr;by region agegr edu sex year;run;

/*Mortality module*/
    /*For children age<15, we use the education of the mother. Therefore,
we pick parameters in a different dataset*/
    data work.pop_survival1;
    merge pop.pop_&styr(in=in1) param.survival_a;
    by region agegr edu sex year;
    if in1;
    run;

(...)

/*Preparing the population file for next period*/
data pop.pop_&endyr;
set work.pop_pop2;

if death=1 then delete;
drop birth dom_mig reclass oldregion oldregion2 region_birth;
run;

/*Generating outputs*/
    /*Population per age sex region and education*/
    proc freq data=pop.pop_&endyr noprint;
    table  year*agegr*sex*edu*region /list norow nocol nopercent nocum
out=work.outputpop(rename=(count=pop) drop=percent);
    weight weight;
    run;

(...)

    /*Merging the population count and components of growth*/
(...)
    data results.output&endyr;
    merge work.outputpop work.birth work.death work.inflow work.outflow
work.gain_urban; work.loss_rural
    by year agegr sex edu region;

    array change _numeric_;
      do over change;
         if change=. then change=0;
         change=round(change);
      end;
    run;
```

We close the macro function with the statement *%mend microsim* right after the last line of the code that needs to be repeated, which is the procedure for cleaning temporary work files.

```
/*Clean temporary dataset*/
proc datasets lib=work kill nolist memtype=data;
quit;

%mend microsim;
```

3.9 Simulating for Next Periods

To run the microsimulation up to 2060, we could call the macro function microsim for every step from 2010 to 2060, for example:

```
%microsim(2010,2015);
%microsim(2015,2020);
(...)
%microsim(2055,2060);
```

Alternatively, since we repeat the macro by increasing parameters by 5 every step, we can imbed a loop function in a second macro (called *loop*) that automatizes the process. Parameters of this macro loop are the initial year of the first and the last step of the projection. When calling the macro using 2010 and 2055 as parameters, the projection will run until 2060 (2055 being the initial year of the last step that thus ends in 2060).

```
%macro loop(first,last);
    %local year;
    %do year = &first %to &last %by 5;
        %microsim (&year, %eval(&year+5))
    %end;
%mend loop;

%loop(2010, 2055);
```

The output of each year is then stored in a specific SAS format dataset (.sas7bdat) in the library *results*, as shown in Fig. 3.10.

To facilitate the analysis of projection outcomes, we can concatenate them together and export the resulting file in CSV. Because we want the initial population of 2010 to be included in the final dataset of results, we first need to create an output for the starting year (2010) having the same format as other outputs for projected years. We thus use the same code, but using "2010" instead of "&styr".

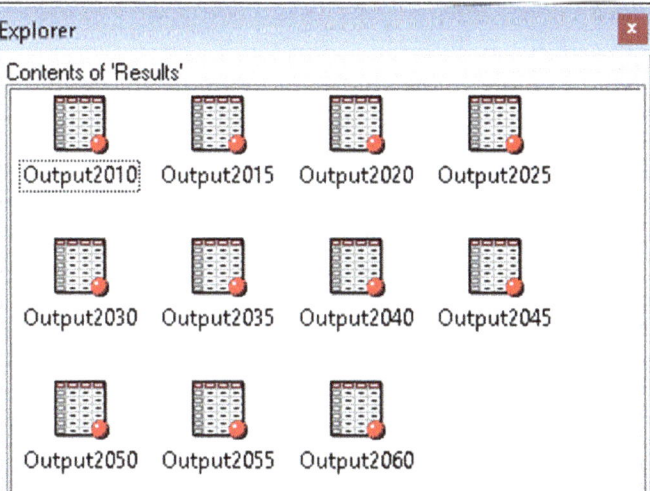

Fig. 3.10 Screenshot of files included in the results library (opened with SAS)

```
/*Population by age sex region education for 2010*/
proc freq data=pop.pop_2010 noprint;
table  year*agegr*sex*edu*region /list norow nocol nopercent nocum
out=results.output2010(rename=(count=pop) drop=percent);
weight weight;
run;

data results.output2010;
set work.output2010;

array change _numeric_;
   do over change;
      if change=. then change=0;
      change=round(change);
   end;
run;
```

In a data step, we then concatenate all files starting with "outputpop" located in the library *results* by using the symbol ':' instead of the year in the dataset name. The resulting file "outputTotal" thus contains the population outcome for all years. Values for components of growth are for the period $t-5$ to t, so they are empty for the year 2010, which is the starting year of the population.

```
/*Concatenating and exporting results*/
data results.outputTotal;
set results.outputpop:;
run;
```

Using the *export* procedure, we can then export the dataset into a CSV file located in the output folder. Personalised tables can then easily be generated with pivot tables from Excel.

```
proc export data=results.outputTotal
outfile=
'C:\Users\Guillaume\Desktop\Microsimulation\&scenario_name\outputs\outputTotal.csv'
dbms=csv
replace;
run;
```

3.10 Validation of Results

The validation of a new model is a necessary step that must be taken before using its outcomes for purposes of analysis. As with any population projection model, the aim of the microsimulation model we built is not to predict what will happen, but rather to forecast the population under conditional assumptions. In our case, those assumptions are taken from another projection model. Therefore, the microsimulation model should reproduce what occurs with that multistate model. In other words, our validation needs to confirm the demographic events are modelled correctly and that there is no error in the code. For this purpose, an external validation by error analysis is sufficient, as it is the most common procedure used to validate population projections (Grummer-Strawn and Espenshade 1991; Smith et al. 2002). If we had built our own assumptions, more sophisticated validation and sensitivity analysis

3.10 Validation of Results

Table 3.1 Error between the multistate and the microsimulation model

Population size of the subgroup	Mean error	Mean absolute error	Mean relative error (%)
[0, 10,000[	−14	942	4
[10,000, 50,000[	−373	5,308	−2
[50,000, 100000[	−916	9,821	−1
[100,000, ∞	−15,131	34,770	−2
All	−3,173	9,122	1

might have been required. For specific examples, see National Research Council (1991) or Caswell and Sánchez Gassen (2015).

We compared our outcomes with those we want to reproduce (the multistate model of KC et al. (2018)). In order to see if there was a systematic bias in the microsimulation model compared to the multistate model, we calculated the mean error and the mean absolute error in the projected population size in 2060 (Table 3.1). We disaggregated the population by the smallest possible comparable subgroups, these being the size of each age-, sex-, education- and region-specific group. We also split results according to the population size of the subgroup. Remember that since the microsimulation is stochastic, results may differ slightly between each run, and consequently, the difference with the multistate model results may also change slightly. We can see that the accuracy of the projection is relatively good, with a mean relative error of 1%. Because of the stochastic nature of the microsimulation, the smaller the population is, the higher the error. Thus, although the mean absolute error when the population size of the subgroup is between 0 and 10,000 is much higher and reaches 4%, it corresponds to a gap of only −14 individuals on average (mean error).

In Fig. 3.11 we compare the projected population by level of education between 2010 and 2060 from our microsimulation model to the outcome from the multistate. The microsimulation leads to very similar results, with a sharp increase in the population between 2010 to 2060 from 1.2 G to almost 1.8 G. Most of the increase is projected to be in the population with an upper secondary or postsecondary level of education, while the population with no education is projected to decline sharply.

In Fig. 3.12, we compare the projected age pyramid by education level in 2060 from each model. In Fig. 3.13, we show the population size by region in 2060. Again, we can observe that the microsimulation produces results similar to those of the multistate projection, though the discrepancy becomes larger for regions with smaller populations, given the Monte Carlo error.

Overall, the microsimulation replicates the multistate model outcomes quite well for broad aggregations, such as the population by age, sex, and education and for subgroups with relatively large populations. However, for more specific subgroups with very small populations, for instance, the men aged 95–99 with postsecondary education in an urban area of Dadra & Nagar Haveli, results may differ dramatically (183 in the multistate vs. 0 in our run of microsimulation). If we are interested in analysing outputs for those small subgroups, we could improve the accuracy of

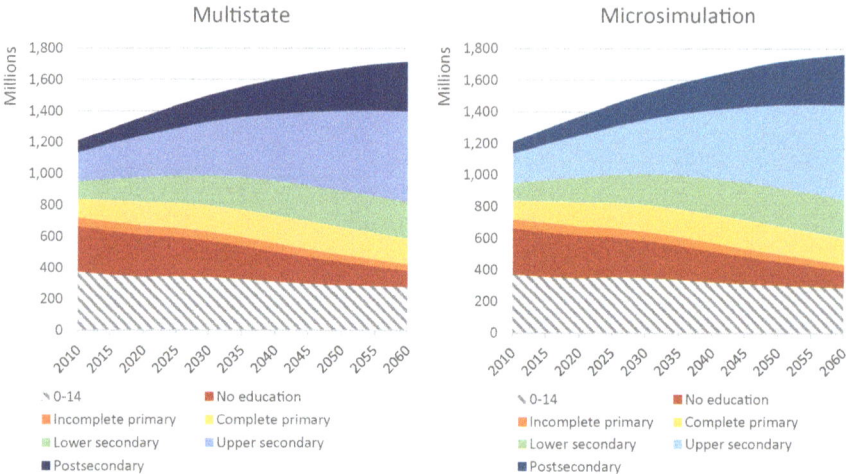

Fig. 3.11 Comparison of projected population size of India by educational attainment from multistate model and microsimulation, 2010–2060

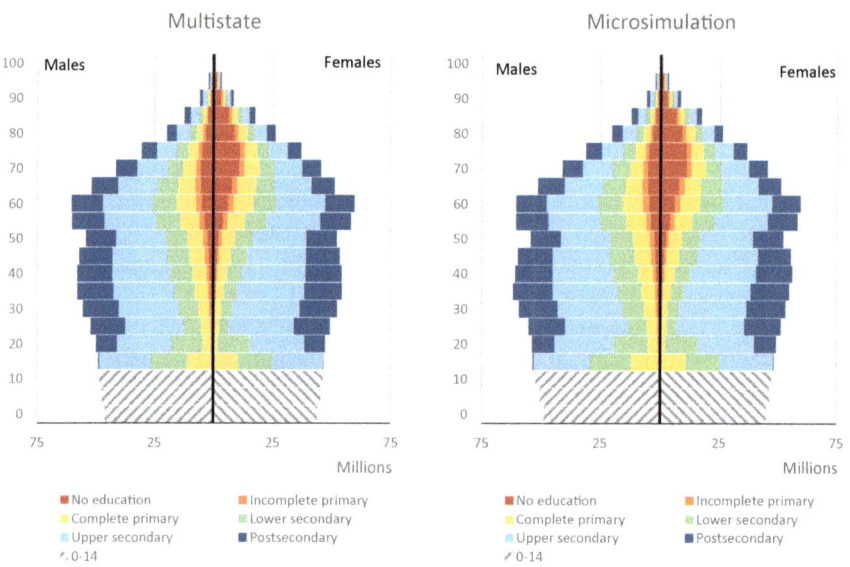

Fig. 3.12 Comparison of the projected age pyramid in 2060 by education in India from multistate model and microsimulation

results by increasing the sample size in the base population. Alternatively, we can also implement some events, such as mortality, using a deterministic approach rather than a stochastic one (see Chap. 6 for details).

3.10 Validation of Results

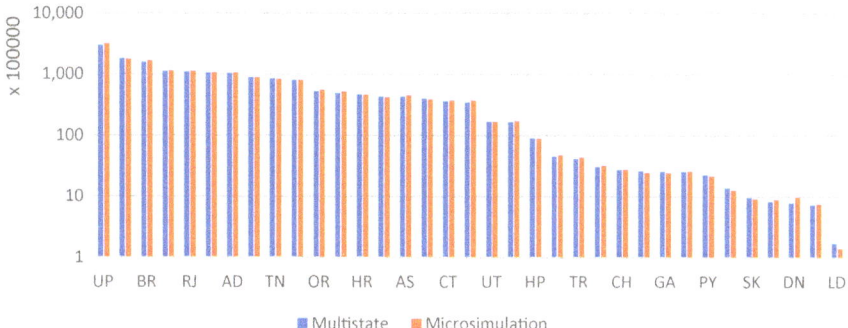

Fig. 3.13 Comparison of the projected population size in 2060 by region, India, from multistate model and microsimulation

References

Caswell, H., & Sánchez Gassen, N. (2015). The sensitivity analysis of population projections. *Demographic Research, 33*, 801–840.

Grummer-Strawn, L., & Espenshade, T. J. (1991). Evaluating the accuracy of U.S. population projection models. In: *Improving information for social policy decisions—the uses of microsimulation modeling.* The National Academies Press, Washington D.C.

Kc, S., Wurzer, M., Speringer, M., & Lutz, W. (2018). Future population and human capital in heterogeneous India. *Proceedings of the National Academy of Sciences of the United States of America, 115*, 8328. https://doi.org/10.1073/pnas.1722359115

National Research Council. (1991). *Improving information for social policy decisions—the uses of microsimulation modeling:* (Vol. I). The National Academies Press, Washington, DC.

Retherford, R. D., & Roy, T. K. (2003). *Factors affecting sex-selective abortion in India and 17 major states.* International Institute for Population Sciences and Honolulu: East-West Center, Mumbai, India

Smith, S. K., Tayman, J., & Swanson, D. A. (2002). *State and local populations projections: Methodology and analysis.* Springer

Open Access This chapter is licensed under the terms of the Creative Commons Attribution 4.0 International License (http://creativecommons.org/licenses/by/4.0/), which permits use, sharing, adaptation, distribution and reproduction in any medium or format, as long as you give appropriate credit to the original author(s) and the source, provide a link to the Creative Commons license and indicate if changes were made.

The images or other third party material in this chapter are included in the chapter's Creative Commons license, unless indicated otherwise in a credit line to the material. If material is not included in the chapter's Creative Commons license and your intended use is not permitted by statutory regulation or exceeds the permitted use, you will need to obtain permission directly from the copyright holder.

Chapter 4
Adding New Dimensions

Abstract This chapter shows how implementing new dimensions into the microsimulation model. As examples, we add two dimensions that can hardly be implemented in a classical projection model: the labour force participation and the sector of activity (formal/informal). Those modules are implemented through statistical modeling using regression parameters. They use as predictors individual characteristics, such as age, sex, region, education, and for women, a binary variable indicating if she gave birth to a child within the last five years. Those two new variables are thus dynamically implemented, as assumptions on fertility have a direct impact on their outcomes.

Keywords Microsimulation · Population projection · Demography · Method · SAS

4.1 Adjusting the Workspace for the Addition of New Dimensions

In Chap. 3, we replicated in a microsimulation framework what a standard multistate model can do. In this chapter, we will increase complexity by adding two dimensions: the labour force participation and the sector of activity. While these variables can be derived from the outcome of a multistate model (e.g. using the resulting population and applying predefined participation rates), the microsimulation can implement them dynamically. In the example, we present in this chapter, the labour force participation and the sector of activity are calculated using parameters from statistical models. Predictors include age/cohort, sex, region of residence, education and a binary variable stating whether the individual is a woman who gave birth within

---

Electronic supplementary material The online version of this chapter (https://doi.org/10.1007/978-3-030-79111-7_4) contains supplementary material, which is available to authorized users.

the last 5 years. As this last predictor suggests, assumptions as to fertility have an impact on the labour force outcome.

The modules for labour force participation and the sector of activity reassess the individual outome of these variables at the end of each period using personal characteristics as determinants. Because of the availability of data used in the statistical model, these modules do not take into account the past labour force participation and sector of activity of the individual. In other words, what is modelled is the probability of being in the labour force rather than the probability of entering or leaving the labour market, or the probability of changing the sector of activity. Consequently, the modeling can project reliable crossectional values, but it does not allow for longitudinal analysis, as life courses may be inconsistent.

The code file "Chapter 4 – Adding new dimensions.sas includes" the complete code of the microsimulation with two additional dimensions that are explained in this chapter. Below, we will explain the difference from the file used in Chap. 3, which replicated a multistate model. First, we change the name of the scenario. In the support documents provided with this book (Chapter ESM), all necessary files can be found in the folder "chapter4".

```
%let scenario_name=Chapter4;
```

The parameter files for modules for labour force participation and the sector of activity were already imported in Chap. 2 (with the macro function *import* and the *sort procedure*). As a reminder, the code lines for this purpose were:

```
%import
("C:\Users\Guillaume\Desktop\Microsimulation\%scenario_name\parameters\
parameters\lfp.csv",param.lfp);
%import
("C:\Users\Guillaume\Desktop\Microsimulation\%scenario_name\parameters\
parameters\formal.csv",param.formal);
%import
("C:\Users\Guillaume\Desktop\Microsimulation\%scenario_name\parameters\
parameters\lfp_imput.csv",param.lfp_imput);
%import
("C:\Users\Guillaume\Desktop\Microsimulation\%scenario_name\parameters\
parameters\formal_imput.csv",param.formal_imput);
```

4.2 Labour Force Participation Module

Labour force participation rates (P) are estimated from a logit regression model. Logit models can be estimated with SAS using the LOGISTIC procedure.[1] When modeling a binary variable such as labour force participation, logit models are preferred over linear models, as the predicted value of a logit model can only range from 0 to 1. If the predicted outcome has more than two categories, multinomial or ordered logit may

---

[1] The documentation for this procedure can be consulted here: https://support.sas.com/documentation/onlinedoc/stat/131/logistic.pdf.

4.2 Labour Force Participation Module

be more appropriate. The logit model used in the labour force participation module is based on data from the National Sample Survey on Employment and Unemployment 2017/2018 (population aged 15–74; n = 323,092). The model is described in Eq. 4.1:

$$\text{logit}(P) = \beta_{s,0} + \beta_{s,1}AGEGR + \beta_{s,2}AGEGR^2 + \beta_{s,3}EDU + \beta_{s,4}REGION + \beta_{s=F,5}YOUNG\_KID + \beta_{s=F,6}POSTSEC * YOUNG\_KID + \beta_{s,7}EDU * AGEGR + \beta_{s,8}EDU * AGEGR^2 \quad (4.1)$$

The logit of a probability corresponds to the natural logarithm of its odds. Therefore, the logit of the participation rate (P) is $\log(P/(1-P))$, and the rate P can be calculated from the parameters, such as:

$$P = \frac{\exp(\beta_{s,0} + \beta_{s,1}AGEGR + \beta_{s,2}AGEGR^2 + \beta_{s,3}EDU + \beta_{s,4}REGION + \beta_{s=F,5}YOUNG\_KID + \beta_{s=F,6}POSTSEC * YOUNG\_KID + \beta_{s,7}EDU * AGEGR + \beta_{s,8}EDU * AGEGR^2)}{1 + \exp(\beta_{s,0} + \beta_{s,1}AGEGR + \beta_{s,2}AGEGR^2 + \beta_{s,3}EDU + \beta_{s,4}REGION + \beta_{s=F,5}YOUNG\_KID + \beta_{s=F,6}POSTSEC * YOUNG\_KID + \beta_{s,7}EDU * AGEGR + \beta_{s,8}EDU * AGEGR^2)} \quad (4.2)$$

Each sex has its own set of parameters and its own intercept. The slope for age, education, and having a young kid is thus assumed to be the same in all regions. The age group is included with a quadratic function, allowing it to be modelled with a reverse U-shape with lower participation rates for younger adults still in school and the elderly. The interaction of age and education allows the model to take into account that the age pattern in labour force participation varies by educational attainment. It was not possible to have region-specific parameters because of the small number of respondents in many categories (such as highly educated people in a specific age range in smaller regions). However, regions have their own gradients.

The max-rescaled R-Square is 0.5342 for the males' model (percent concordant = 91.2) and 0.2374 for the females' one (percent concordant = 76.6). Complete parameters can be found in the parameters file lfp. In Fig. 4.1, we showed the predicted rates from the model by age and education for both males and females (with no young kid). For males, rates are very high for everyone between 25 and 59. The education gap concerns mainly young and older adults, with lower rates for higher educated ones. In other words, more educated men enter later in the labour market, since they stay at school longer, and they also retire earlier, probably because they have better jobs during their working lives and can afford an earlier retirement. For females, the pattern is very different. For all education categories and at any age groups, rates are much lower than for men, generally more than twice as low. Furthermore, the effect of education seems to follow a U-shape, with higher rates for both the highest and lowest categories. These trends are similar to those observed by Kapsos et al. (2014).

The parameter for the variable young_kid is −0.3236, implying that women who gave birth within the last 5 years are much less likely to work. This parameter would thus reduce by about 8.5 percentage points a participation rate that would otherwise have been 42%. The negative impact of having a young_kid is moreover much larger

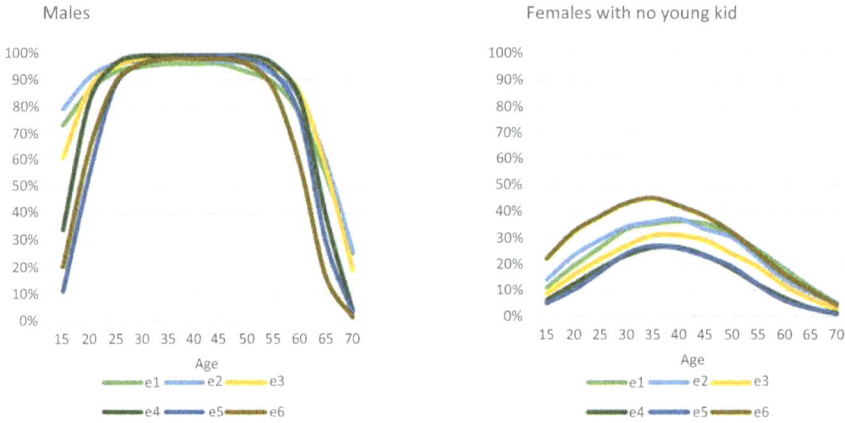

Fig. 4.1 Predicted labour force participation rates from Eq. 4.1 by age and education, India

for women with a postsecondary education than for other women, as the parameter for the interaction between these two variables is −0.3895. Finally, parameters show strong heterogeneity among regions, and also higher participation rates in rural areas than in urban areas of the same region.

For other modules, assumptions are implemented directly as rates that were merged to individuals according to their characteristics. For the labour force participation module, we use regression parameters and therefore, the implementation method is different. Variable-specific parameters will first be merged one by one to the corresponding population. Then, using those parameters, we will calculate the individual probability of participating in the labour force.

To merge the parameter file to the population file, we need to structure it in a particular way, as shown in Fig. 4.2. Each discrete variable needs to have its own column with specific categories on different rows. Parameters corresponding to these categories are on another column, under the label 'variable name'_p. Reference categories (such as edu = e3) also need to be included with a parameter of 0. Otherwise, a missing value would be used in the calculation of the rate, which would result in an error. For continuous variables as well as for intercepts, since they are applied in the calculation of the labour force participation rate for each individual, each is implemented under a specific column, such as agegr_p and agegr2_p for the two parameters of the quadratic form of age, and agegr_edu_p and agegr_edu_p for the quadratic form of the interaction of age with education.

The labour force participation module is implemented once the demographic events are completed, when the age and year are those corresponding to the end of the period. The population file to be used is thus work.pop2 and the module needs to be written right after the "time module" and before cleaning the population file for the next period.

4.2 Labour Force Participation Module

sex	edu	young_kid	region	intercept	edu_p	agegr_p	agegr2_p	agegr_edu_p	agegr2_edu_p	young_kid_p	young_kid_edu_p	region_p
1				-4.4198								
1		0								0		
1		1									-0.3236	
1	e1				0.3929							
1	e2				0.9207							
1	e3				0							
1	e4				-1.5251							
1	e5				-2.3395							
1	e6				1.0876							
1						0.1847						
1							-0.00248					
1	e1							0.000397				
1	e2							-0.0266				
1	e3							0				
1	e4							0.0685				
1	e5							0.1092				
1	e6							-0.00883				
1	e1								0.000007265			
1	e2								0.000251			
1	e3								0			
1	e4								-0.00087			
1	e5								-0.00133			
1	e6								0.000007983			
1	e1	0										0
1	e2	0										0
1	e3	0										0
1	e4	0										0
1	e5	0										0
1	e6	0										0
1	e1	1										0
1	e2	1										0
1	e3	1										0
1	e4	1										0
1	e5	1										0
1	e6	1										-0.3895

Fig. 4.2 Screenshot of the parameter file lfp.csv (opened with Excel)

First, we need to merge the parameters file (param.lfp) with the population file (pop2). Using the merge statement as in previous modules would not be optimal, since it would require a specific merging for each variable from the logit model. We thus use a command in Structured Query Language (SQL),[2] which is supported by SAS. We create a new population file (pop_lfp1) that links parameters from the file lfp to individuals for the last population file (pop2, that we select under p.*). Parameters are selected one by one, with the appropriate variables (under t1 to t9). Parameters in each set are joined by their specific correspondent variables. For instance, parameters for education are joined both by sex and education, while parameters for the presence of kids and its interaction with education are joined by sex, education, and presence of kids, and so on for other sets of parameters. In the code, we also specify "where not missing ('name of the parameter)" to join only the values of parameters, as we don't want missing cells to be imported.

---

[2] For more information about using SQL in SAS, see: https://support.sas.com/resources/papers/proceedings/proceedings/sugi30/257-30.pdf.

```sas
/*Labor force participation*/
  /*Implementing parameters*/
proc sql;
  create table pop_lfp1 as
    select
      p.*,
      t1.intercept, t2.edu_p, t3.agegr_p, t4.agegr2_p, t5.agegr_edu_p,
      t6.agegr2_edu_p, t7.young_kid_p, t8.young_kid_edu_p, t9.region_p

    from
      pop2 p

      left join
      ( select sex, intercept
        from param.lfp
        where not missing(intercept)
      ) t1
      on p.sex=t1.sex

      left join
      ( select sex, edu, edu_p
        from param.lfp
        where not missing(edu_p)
      ) t2
      on p.sex=t2.sex and p.edu=t2.edu

      left join
      ( select sex, agegr_p
        from param.lfp
        where not missing(agegr_p)
      ) t3
      on p.sex=t3.sex

      left join
      ( select sex, agegr2_p
        from param.lfp
        where not missing(agegr2_p)
      ) t4
      on p.sex=t4.sex

      left join
      ( select sex, edu, agegr_edu_p
        from param.lfp
        where not missing(agegr_edu_p)
      ) t5
      on p.sex=t5.sex and p.edu=t5.edu

      left join
      ( select sex, edu, agegr2_edu_p
        from param.lfp
        where not missing(agegr2_edu_p)
      ) t6
      on p.sex=t6.sex and p.edu=t6.edu

      left join
      ( select sex, young_kid, young_kid_p
        from param.lfp
        where not missing(young_kid_p)
      ) t7
      on p.sex=t7.sex and p.young_kid=t7.young_kid
```

4.2 Labour Force Participation Module

```
           left join
           ( select sex, edu, young_kid, young_kid_edu_p
             from param.lfp
             where not missing(young_kid_edu_p)
           )t8
           on p.sex=t8.sex and p.edu=t8.edu and p.young_kid=t8.young_kid
           left join
           ( select sex, region, region_p
             from param.lfp
             where not missing(region_p)
           )t9
           on p.sex=t9.sex and p.region=t9.region;
quit;
```

The population file pop_lfp1 now includes individual-specific parameters for the labour force participation module. Starting from this file, we create a new one (pop_lfp2) in which the labour force participation event occurs. For each step of the projection, the labour force variable is first reset to 0 (out of the labour force) for all individuals (labour = 0). We then calculate the individual-specific labour force participation rate for the population affected by the event (those aged between 15 and 74). In our example, we use logit regression parameters. The rate thus corresponds to the exponential of the sum of parameters (multiplied by the value of the variable in the case of continuous variables) divided by 1 + the exponential of the sum parameters.

```
        /*Labour force participation event*/
        data work.pop_lfp2;
        set work.pop_lfp1;

        labour=0;
        if 15<=agegr<74 then do;
          exp_lab = exp(intercept + agegr_p*agegr + agegr2_p*agegr*agegr + edu_p
    + agegr_edu_p*agegr + agegr2_edu_p*agegr*agegr
          + region_p + young_kid_p + young_kid_edu_p);
          prob_lab = exp_lab/(1+exp_lab);
        (…)
```

Once each individual has a specific probability of participating in the labour force, we can proceed to the simulation of the event with the Monte Carlo method. When the rate is higher than the random number, we switch the labour force variable to 1. Finally, we drop parameters for labour force participation from the population file.

```
        (…)
           if rand('uniform')<prob_lab then labour=1;
           end;

           drop intercept agegr_p edu_p agegr_edu_p agegr2_p agegr2_edu_p
        region_p young_kid_p young_kid_edu_p exp_lab prob_lab;
           run;
```

4.3 Sector of Activity Module

In India, as in many developing countries, the informal sector (jobs that are not regulated or monitored by the government, including unpaid jobs) represents a large part of the economy. With the modernisation of the economy, urbanisation, globalisation, the demographic transition, and the expansion of the educational attainment, the informal sector is likely to shrink and be replaced by formal jobs (Cáceres-Delpiano 2012; McCaig and Pavcnik 2015; Siggel 2010).

The sector of activity module is implemented in the same way as the labour force participation module, with logit regression parameters. However, covariates and their interactions differ. More than age, the cohort of birth has a major influence on whether or not an individual is likely to work in the formal sector (McCaig and Pavcnik 2015). Thus, the formalisation of an economy occurs in large part by the replacement of generations, through the mechanism of demographic metabolism (Lutz 2013). Accordingly, the modelling of the sector of activity (S) uses the cohort of birth as an individual determinant, while the age dimension is dismissed. Equation 4.3 describes the model:

$$\text{logit}(S) = SEX * (\beta_0 + \beta_1 COHORT + \beta_2 EDU + \beta_3 REGION + \beta_4 YOUNG\_KID + \beta_5 POST\_SEC * YOUNG\_KID + \beta_6 REGION * COHORT) \quad (4.3)$$

The model is applied only to the active population of the National Sample Survey on Employment and Unemployment 2017/2018. The max-rescaled R-Square is 0.3080 for the males' model (percent concordant = 78.3) and 0.5235 for the females' model (percent concordant = 88.4). Complete parameters can be found in the parameters file *formal*. As for the labour force participation model, each sex has its own set of parameters and its own intercept.

The cohort is implemented as a continuous variable taking the value of 0 for the cohort born in 1940–1944, 1 for those born in 1945–1949 and so on. The cohort parameter thus captures the secular trend that can be extrapolated for future cohorts entering the labour market. The model also includes an interaction between the cohort and the region in order to take into account the regional disparity in the pace of development. To avoid inconsistencies for regions that already have a very high proportion of the active population working in the formal sector, we added the constraint that region-specific cohort trends need to be positive or equal to 0 ($\beta_1 + \beta_6 \geq 0$).

In Fig. 4.3, we present the extrapolation for future cohorts of the arithmetic average (not weighted by region population) of region-specific cohort parameters. It shows that for both sexes, there is a sharply increasing trend in the proportion of workers in the formal sector. A bit more than 20% of cohorts born in the 50s work in the formal sector, compared to half of cohorts born in the late 90s. When extrapolating trends, the proportions will exceed 60% for cohorts born after 2025. Despite having much lower labour force participation rates, women are slightly more likely to work in the formal sector, but the gap will gradually close. The model also accounts for strong

4.3 Sector of Activity Module

regional differentials (not shown in the figure). Rates are in general much lower in rural regions than in urban ones, but the difference shrinks gradually over cohorts.

In addition to cohort and region, the model also includes education, a parameter for women that have a young child (having given birth in the last 5 years) and its interaction with the education. As shown in Table 4.1, presenting odds ratios for the educational attainment, education emerges as a key determinant of having a formal job for both males and females, as a steep gradient in parameters is observed between the lowest degree and the highest. Active men with a postsecondary education are about 10 times more likely to work in the formal sector than men with no education (6.699/0.544). This ratio is above 25 for women (17.921/0.689).

Finally, the model includes the negative effect of having a young kid at home for women on the probability of working in the formal sector (−0.845). The positive parameter (0.799) for the interaction of the variables YOUNG_KID and POST_SEC

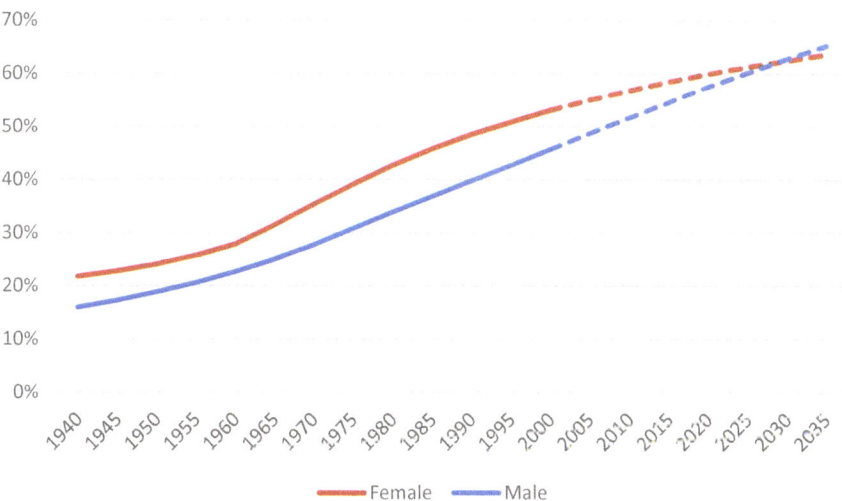

Fig. 4.3 Arithmetic average of region-specific cohort parameters for the sector of activity converted into rate (education = complete primary; no birth in the last 5 years)

Table 4.1 Odds of working in the formal sector by level of educational attainment ($\exp(\beta_2)$ from Eq. 4.3)

Educational attainment	Males	Females
e1—No education	0.654[a]	0.689[a]
e2—Incomplete primary	0.823[a]	0.885
e3—Complete primary	1.000	1.000
e4—Lower secondary	1.370[a]	1.603[a]
e5—Upper secondary	2.168[a]	3.881[a]
e6—Postsecondary	6.699[a]	17.921[a]

[a]<0.0001

Source Authors' calculations from the National Sample Survey on Employment and Unemployment 2017/2018

however suggests that this effect is much less for women with a postsecondary education.

As the sector of activity module also uses regression coefficients, the parameter file "formal" has the same format as the parameter "lfp file" (one different column for each variable and one different column for each set of parameters), as shown in Fig. 4.4. As a reminder, the cohort is implemented as a continuous variable and therefore does not require a category to link it to the corresponding population.

The code to implement parameters is also similar to the one used for the labour force participation module. Using a SQL command, in a new population file called "pop_formal1", we join to the last population file ("pop_lfp2") the parameters from the parameters file "formal" (which is stored in the library *param*), using the appropriate set of variables for each parameter.

	A	B	C	D	E	F	G	H	I	J	K
1	sex	edu	young_kid	region	intercept	edu_p	cohort_p	young_kid_p	young_kid_edu_p	region_p	cohort_region_p
2	1				-0.2422						
3	1		0					0			
4	1		1					-0.845			
5	1	e1				-0.373					
6	1	e2				-0.1217					
7	1	e3				0					
8	1	e4				0.4722					
9	1	e5				1.3562					
10	1	e6				2.8855					
11	1	e1	0						0		
12	1	e2	0						0		
13	1	e3	0						0		
14	1	e4	0						0		
15	1	e5	0						0		
16	1	e6	0						0		
17	1	e1	1						0		
18	1	e2	1						0		
19	1	e3	1						0		
20	1	e4	1						0		
21	1	e5	1						0		
22	1	e6	1						0.7992		
23	1						0.00458				
24	1			AD_rural						-2.3663	
25	1			AD_urban						-0.2655	
26	1			AN_rural						-2.0301	
27	1			AN_urban						-0.622	
28	1			AR_rural						-4.1565	

Fig. 4.4 Screenshot of the parameter file formal.csv (opened with Excel)

4.3 Sector of Activity Module

```
/*Sector of activity*/
    /*Implementing parameters*/
    proc sql;
        create table pop_formal1 as
            select
                p.*,
                t1.intercept, t2.edu_p, t3.cohort_p, t4.cohort_region_p,
                t5.young_kid_p, t6.young_kid_edu_p, t7.region_p

            from
                pop_lfp2 p

            left join
            ( select sex, intercept
              from param.formal
              where not missing(intercept)
            ) t1
            on p.sex=t1.sex

            left join
            ( select sex, edu, edu_p
              from param.formal
              where not missing(edu_p)
            ) t2
            on p.sex=t2.sex and p.edu=t2.edu

            left join
            ( select sex, cohort_p
              from param.formal
              where not missing(cohort_p)
            ) t3
            on p.sex=t3.sex

        left join
        ( select sex, region, cohort_region_p
          from param.formal
          where not missing(cohort_region_p)
        ) t4
        on p.sex=t4.sex and p.region=t4.region

        left join
        ( select sex, young_kid, young_kid_p
          from param.formal
          where not missing(young_kid_p)
        ) t5
        on p.sex=t5.sex and p.young_kid=t5.young_kid

        left join
        ( select sex, edu, young_kid, young_kid_edu_p
          from param.formal
          where not missing(young_kid_edu_p)
        ) t6
        on p.sex=t6.sex and p.edu=t6.edu and p.young_kid=t6.young_kid

        left join
        ( select sex, region, region_p
          from param.formal
          where not missing(region_p)
        ) t7
        on p.sex=t7.sex and p.region=t7.region;
quit;
```

In a new population file (pop_formal2), we can now simulate the event, which will split workers between the formal and the informal sector. First, in a temporary variable "cohort2", we need to transform the cohort variable to make it correspond to the one used in the regression model. As a reminder, the cohort born in 1940–1944 has the value 0, while the cohort born in 1945–1949 has the value 1, and so on. Therefore, the cohort variable used in the sector of activity event should be (cohort—1940)/5. Someone born in 2020 would thus have a value of 16.

```
/*Formal - Informal event*/
data work.pop_formal2;
set work.pop_formal1;

cohort2=(cohort-1940)/5;
(…)
```

Because the sector of activity is modelled using a cross-sectional approach, we reset the variable to 0 (formal = 0, which corresponds to being out of the labour force). For those aged 15 to 74 and in the labour force (labour = 1, which is the outcome of the labour force module of the previous section), we set by default the variable formal to 1, signifying working in the informal sector. We then use parameters to calculate the probability of working in the formal sector (prob_form) and we proceed to the Monte Carlo experiment to select those who work in the formal sector (formal = 2). Finally, we drop parameters and temporary variables.

```
    (…)

    formal=0;
    if 15<=agegr<74 and labour=1 then do;
    formal=1;
    if (cohort_region_p+cohort_p)<0 then do; cohort_region_p=0; cohort_p=0;end;
    exp_form = exp(intercept + edu_p + cohort2*cohort_p + cohort2*cohort_region_
p + region_p + young_kid_p + young_kid_edu_p);
    prob_form = exp_form/(1+exp_form);
    if rand('uniform')<prob_form then formal=2;
    end;

    drop intercept cohort_p edu_p cohort_region_p region_p young_kid_p young
_kid_edu_p exp_form prob_form cohort2
    run;
```

Now, the last population file is work.pop_formal2. In the section for cleaning the population file for the next period, we thus need to replace pop2 (which was the last population file in Chap. 3) with this.

```
/*Cleaning the population file for next period*/
data pop.pop_&endyr;
set work.pop_formal2;
(…)
```

4.4 Including the New Dimensions in the Outputs

The population file pop_&endyr (pop_2015 for the first step of the projection) now includes the projected status of the labour force and the projected sector of activity. We now need to modify the code that generates the projection outputs to include these dimensions. First, in the code generating the population by some characteristics, we add the variable "formal" to the table.

4.4 Including the New Dimensions in the Outputs

```
/*Generating outputs*/
   /*Population per age sex region education and lfp*/
   proc freq data=pop.pop_&endyr noprint;
   table year*agegr*sex*edu*region*formal/list norow nocol nopercent nocum
out=work.outputpop(rename=(count=pop) drop=percent);
   weight weight;
   run;
```

The variable for labour force participation (labour) doesn't need to be included, since it can be rebuilt from the variable "formal" (summing up those working in the formal sector and those working in the informal sector gives the active population, while the inactive have their own category).

After adding this new dimension to the outputpop table, each set of age-sex-region-education group is now divided into three categories, "inactive" (formal = 0), "working in the informal sector" (formal = 1) and "working in the formal sector" (formal = 2), as illustrated in Fig. 4.5, showing a screenshot of the file.

Before merging the population count with the components of the growth, we need to transpose the output file "outputpop" that we just created to have the variable "pop" in three columns, one for each category of the variable "formal". We use the transpose procedure for this purpose. The variable "pop" is selected following the statement var which selects the variable to transpose. The "by" statement identifies the group of variables in columns in the new dataset. We specify the variable "formal" under the "id" statement to have one column for each category of this variable. Since a column cannot have numerical label, an underscore is added, so the category 0 is labelled as _0, 1 as _1 and 2 as _2. In the options of the out statement, we rename the new columns by the name of the category, "inactive" for _0, "informal" for _1, and "formal" for _2.

	YEAR	agegr	SEX	edu	region	formal	Frequency Count
1	2015	0	0	0 e1	AD_rural	0	2235137.529
2	2015	5	0	0 e1	AD_rural	0	2038141.1602
3	2015	10	0	0 e1	AD_rural	0	2475631.3676
4	2015	15	0	0 e1	AD_rural	0	58334.388955
5	2015	15	0	0 e1	AD_rural	1	104373.21069
6	2015	15	0	0 e1	AD_rural	2	9647.7334567
7	2015	20	0	0 e1	AD_rural	0	53090.154745
8	2015	20	0	0 e1	AD_rural	1	197626.53589
9	2015	20	0	0 e1	AD_rural	2	36418.005977
10	2015	25	0	0 e1	AD_rural	0	38742.808237
11	2015	25	0	0 e1	AD_rural	1	418318.91639
12	2015	25	0	0 e1	AD_rural	2	32774.619467
13	2015	30	0	0 e1	AD_rural	0	30559.077893
14	2015	30	0	0 e1	AD_rural	1	548744.2201
15	2015	30	0	0 e1	AD_rural	2	68537.10778

Fig. 4.5 Screenshot of outputpop before the transpose procedure

	YEAR	agegr	SEX	edu	region	inactive	informal	formal
1	2015	0	0	e1	AD_rural	2235137.529		
2	2015	5	0	e1	AD_rural	2038141.1602		
3	2015	10	0	e1	AD_rural	2475631.3676		
4	2015	15	0	e1	AD_rural	58334.388955	104373.21069	9647.7334567
5	2015	20	0	e1	AD_rural	53090.154745	197626.53589	36418.005977
6	2015	25	0	e1	AD_rural	38742.808237	418318.91639	32774.619467
7	2015	30	0	e1	AD_rural	30559.077893	548744.2201	68537.10778
8	2015	35	0	e1	AD_rural	10000	638533.45225	56356.786126
9	2015	40	0	e1	AD_rural	6127.869963	716163.72669	74615.186103
10	2015	45	0	e1	AD_rural	36495.024978	740170.11632	95762.205042
11	2015	50	0	e1	AD_rural	48183.353386	713048.16198	27001.847059
12	2015	55	0	e1	AD_rural	69613.374308	550573.27157	25498.987941
13	2015	60	0	e1	AD_rural	150245.30838	312995.70141	14254.91057
14	2015	65	0	e1	AD_rural	291316.30947	271673.92933	22035.514926
15	2015	70	0	e1	AD_rural	234398.90857	84293.580827	473.68696612
16	2015	75	0	e1	AD_rural	287001.29061		

Fig. 4.6 Screenshot of outputpop after the transpose procedure

```
proc transpose data=work.outputpop out=work.outputpop (rename=(
_0=inactive _1=informal _2=formal)drop=_name_ _label_);
var pop;
by year agegr sex edu region;
id formal;
run;
```

An excerpt of the resulting dataset is shown in Fig. 4.6. Values are indeed missing in the formal and informal columns for the age group 0–14 and 75+, as by default in the modelling, they are all inactive.

The merger with the components of growth outputs can then proceed. However, the population is still split among the inactive, the informal workers, and the formal workers. In the code that creates the final output file of the period (output_&endyr), we can rebuild the total population and the active population, right after changing the missing values into 0 and the rounding of outcomes. As highlighted in yellow in the code below, the active population thus corresponds to the sum of the formal and informal workers, while the total population (pop) corresponds to the sum of the inactive and active populations.

```
/*Merging the population count and components of growth*/
(...)
data results.output&endyr;
merge work.outputpop work.birth work.death work.inflow work.outflow;
by year agegr sex edu region;

array change _numeric_;
  do over change;
     if change=. then change=0;
     change=round(change);
  end;

active=formal+informal;
pop=inactive+active;
run;
```

Up to this point, the labour force participation and the sector of activity have been projected from 2015 to 2060, but they are not included in the initial population of

4.4 Including the New Dimensions in the Outputs

2010. Since we want to be able to generate trends, we need to incorporate those variables in the initial population. Ideally, we would use real values from a survey, such as the National Sample Survey on Employment and Unemployment 2009, but the variable suffered from methodological problems in this wave and is therefore not comparable (Kapsos et al. 2014). We will thus input those variables in the initial population in a way similar to what we did for the forecasted years, using regression parameters from the National Sample Survey on Employment and Unemployment 2017/2018.

Because the initial population does not include a variable on the presence of a child in the model, we need to re-estimate the logit models without this variable. Those parameters are included in the parameter files lfp_imput.csv and formal_imput.csv, which were imported and converted already in Chap. 2. Parameters for men are exactly those used for the simulation, while those for women differ slightly because of the omission of the presence of a child at home in the model. The structure of these files is the same as those used for the simulation, with each variable having its own column with their specific categories on different rows and parameters corresponding to these categories in another column.

We impute the labour force and sector of activity to the base population of 2010 the same way we did for the simulation, with SQL commands that first merge individuals to parameters corresponding to their characteristics. For the labour force, this is done in a temporary population dataset "lfp_imput".

```
/*Imputing the labour force participation and the sector of activity for 2010*/
   /*Labour force participation*/
   /*Implementing parameters*/
   proc sql;
   create table work.lfp_imput as
     select
       p.*,
       t1.intercept, t2.edu_p, t3.agegr_p, t4.agegr2_p, t5.agegr_edu_p,
       t6.agegr2_edu_p, t7.region_p

     from
      pop.pop_2010 p

       left join
       ( select sex, intercept
         from param.lfp_imput
         where not missing(intercept)
       ) t1
       on p.sex=t1.sex

       left join
       ( select sex, edu, edu_p
         from param.lfp_imput
         where not missing(edu_p)
       ) t2
       on p.sex=t2.sex and p.edu=t2.edu

       left join
       ( select sex, agegr_p
         from param.lfp
         where not missing(agegr_p)
       ) t3
       on p.sex=t3.sex
```

```sas
    left join
    ( select sex, agegr2_p
      from param.lfp
      where not missing(agegr2_p)
    )t4
    on p.sex=t4.sex

    left join
    ( select sex, edu, agegr_edu_p
      from param.lfp_imput
      where not missing(agegr_edu_p)
    )t5
    on p.sex=t5.sex and p.edu=t5.edu

    left join
    ( select sex, edu, agegr2_edu_p
      from param.lfp_imput
      where not missing(agegr2_edu_p)
    )t6
    on p.sex=t6.sex and p.edu=t6.edu

    left join
    ( select sex, region, region_p
      from param.lfp_imput
      where not missing(region_p)
    )t7
    on p.sex=t7.sex and p.region=t7.region;
quit;
```

From this, the imputation is then done with a random experiment in a data step creating a new population dataset "lfp_imput2".

```sas
    /*Labour force participation imputation*/
    data work.lfp_imput2;
    set work.lfp_imput;

    labour=0;
    if 15<=agegr<74 then do;
        exp_lab = exp(intercept + agegr_p*agegr + agegr2_p*agegr*agegr + edu_p +
    agegr_edu_p*agegr + agegr2_edu_p*agegr*agegr
        + region_p);
        prob_lab = exp_lab/(1+exp_lab);

        if rand('uniform')<prob_lab then labour=1;
    end;

    drop intercept agegr_p edu_p agegr_edu_p agegr2_p agegr2_edu_p region_p
        exp_lab prob_lab;
    run;
```

The same is then done for the sector of activity. The resulting dataset "formal_imput2" includes the base population of 2010 with their imputed labour force participation and sector of activity.

4.4 Including the New Dimensions in the Outputs

```
/*Sector of activity*/
/*Implementing parameters*/
proc sql;
  create table work.formal_imput as
    select
      p.*,
      t1.intercept, t2.edu_p, t3.cohort_p, t4.cohort_region_p,
      t5.region_p

    from
      work.lfp_imput2 p

      left join
      ( select sex, intercept
        from param.formal_imput
        where not missing(intercept)
      ) t1
      on p.sex=t1.sex

      left join
      ( select sex, edu, edu_p
        from param.formal_imput
        where not missing(edu_p)
      ) t2
      on p.sex=t2.sex and p.edu=t2.edu

      left join
      ( select sex, cohort_p
        from param.formal_imput
        where not missing(cohort_p)
      ) t3
      on p.sex=t3.sex


      left join
      ( select sex, region, cohort_region_p
        from param.formal_imput
        where not missing(cohort_region_p)
      ) t4
      on p.sex=t4.sex and p.region=t4.region

      left join
      ( select sex, region, region_p
        from param.formal_imput
        where not missing(region_p)
      ) t5
      on p.sex=t5.sex and p.region=t5.region;
  quit;

  /*Formal - Informal imputation*/
  data work.formal_imput2;
  set work.formal_imput;

  cohort2=(cohort-1940)/5;

  formal=0;
  if 15<=agegr<74 and labour=1 then do;
  formal=1;
  if (cohort_region_p+cohort_p)<0 then do; cohort_region_p=0; cohort_p=0;end;
  exp_form = exp(intercept + edu_p + cohort2*cohort_p + cohort2*cohort_region_p
  + region_p);prob_form = exp_form/(1+exp_form);
  if rand('uniform')<prob_form then formal=2;
  end;

  drop intercept cohort_p edu_p cohort_region_p region_p exp_form prob_form cohort2;
  run;
```

Before concatenating the output files of the different periods together, we apply the same addition (highlighted in yellow) in the code of the imputed population of 2010 as we did for the simulated population, in order to have five columns for population count in the output: the total population, the active one, those working in the formal sector, those working in the informal one and those who are inactive.

```
*Population by age sex region education for 2010*/
proc freq data=pop.formal_imput2 noprint;
table   year*agegr*sex*edu*region*formal/list norow nocol nopercent nocum
out=work.output2010(rename=(count=pop) drop=percent);
weight weight;
run;

proc transpose data=work.output2010 out=work.output2010(rename=(_0=inactive
=inactive _1=informal _2=formal) drop=_name_ _label_);
var pop;
by year agegr sex edu region;
id formal;
run;

data results.output2010;
set work.output2010;

array change _numeric_;
   do over change;
       if change=. then change=0;
       change=round(change);
   end;
active=formal+informal;
pop=inactive+active;

run;
```

The final output file exported in CSV (outputTotal.csv) now includes the population by age, sex, education, region, labour force status and sector of activity.

4.5 Overview of Results

The scenario produced in this chapter assumes constant parameters for labour force participation and sector of activity. At aggregated levels, this means that any change in those dimensions comes from changes in the population composition. In Fig. 4.7, we show the projection outcomes by labour force status and sector of activity.

The total population of India is projected to grow by a bit more than 500 M from 2010 to 2060. About 40% (210 M) of this growth will be among the active population (formal + informal), which is likely to stabilize around 2045, passing from about 415 M in 2010 to 625 M. Accordingly, the labour force dependency ratio (the inactive population divided by the active one) will not change much over the next decades. According to this scenario, a small decline may first be seen as a result of the demographic dividend. The ratio will thus pass from about 1.93 in 2010 to

4.5 Overview of Results

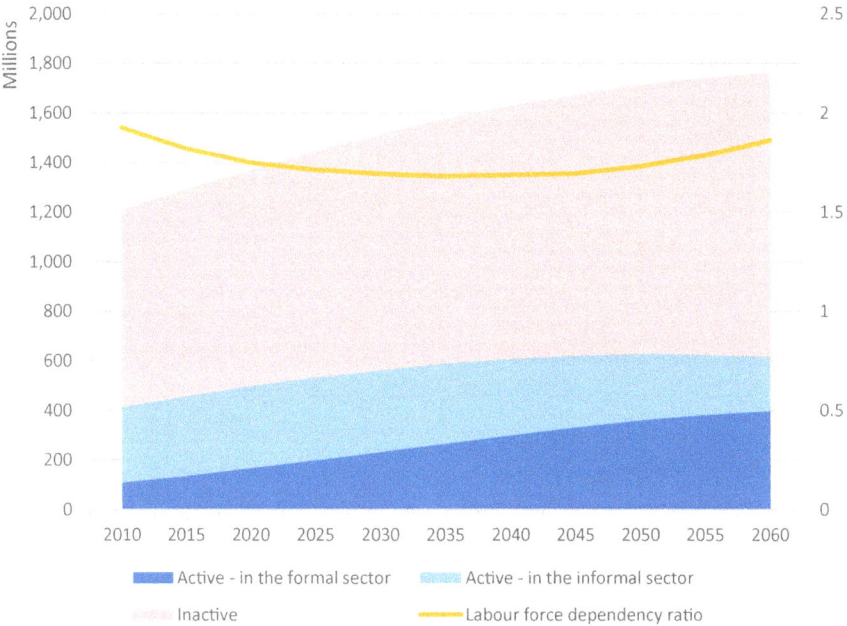

Fig. 4.7 Projected population by labour force status and sector of activity (left) and labour force dependency ratio (right), India, 2010–2060

1.68 in 2040. Because of the population ageing that will further increase the share of elderly that are inactive, the ratio will then increase slightly, reaching 1.86 in 2060.

The composition of the labour force will however change drastically. In 2010, about one quarter of workers worked in the formal sector. This proportion is likely to grow to 65% in 2060. This change is caused by a cohort effect. By demographic metabolism, the younger cohorts that are already much more likely to work in the formal sector will gradually replace the older ones.

As shown in Fig. 4.8, the education composition of the labour force is also projected to change drastically. The proportion of workers with a high school degree or above is likely to double, passing from about one-third in 2010 to about two-third in 2060. The proportion of women among workers, however, remains very low (about 20%). This is because of our assumption of constant parameters. This means that India doesn't use a large portion of its potential workforce, and therefore, the projected labour force size and the labour force dependency ratio could be much better. In the next chapter, we will build an alternative scenario showing what India might gain from greater participation of women in the labour force.

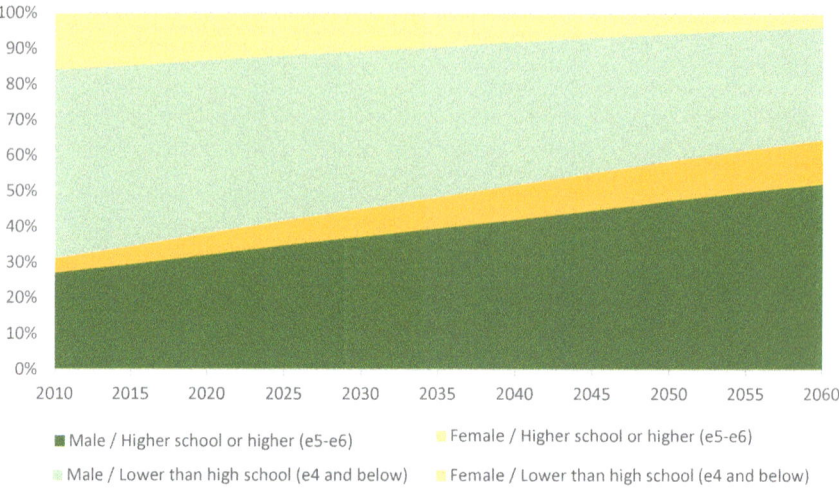

Fig. 4.8 Projected change in the sex and education composition of the labour force, India, 2010–2060

References

Cáceres-Delpiano, J. (2012). Can we still learn something from the relationship between fertility and mother's employment? Evidence from developing countries. *Demography, 49*, 151–174. https://doi.org/10.1007/s13524-011-0076-6

Kapsos, S., Silberman, A., & Bourmpoula, E. (2014). Why is female labour force participation declining so sharply in India. International Labour Office, Geneva, Switzerland.

Lutz, W. (2013). Demographic metabolism: A predictive theory of socioeconomic change. *Population and Development Review, 38*, 283–301. https://doi.org/10.1111/j.1728-4457.2013.00564.x

McCaig, B., & Pavcnik, N. (2015). Informal employment in a growing and globalizing low-income country. *American Economic Review, 105*, 545–550. https://doi.org/10.1257/aer.p20151051

Siggel, E. (2010). The Indian informal sector: The impact of globalization and reform. *International Labour Review, 149*, 93–105. https://doi.org/10.1111/j.1564-913X.2010.00077.x

Open Access This chapter is licensed under the terms of the Creative Commons Attribution 4.0 International License (http://creativecommons.org/licenses/by/4.0/), which permits use, sharing, adaptation, distribution and reproduction in any medium or format, as long as you give appropriate credit to the original author(s) and the source, provide a link to the Creative Commons license and indicate if changes were made.

The images or other third party material in this chapter are included in the chapter's Creative Commons license, unless indicated otherwise in a credit line to the material. If material is not included in the chapter's Creative Commons license and your intended use is not permitted by statutory regulation or exceeds the permitted use, you will need to obtain permission directly from the copyright holder.

Chapter 5
Building Alternative Scenarios

Abstract New dimensions added in the projection models in Chap. 4, the labour force participation and the sector of activity, are modelled using regression parameters. In this chapter, we show how building alternative scenarios with this type of inputs. In the first example, we test an assumption in which women with young children at home have the same participation rate as other women. The second example, we test a scenario in which labour force participation rates of women gradually increase and reach those of men by 2060. The code to implement those alternative scenarios is explained, and some results are presented.

Keywords Microsimulation · Population projection · Demography · Method · SAS

5.1 Building Alternative Scenarios from Regression Parameters

At this point, we have replicated a reference scenario for a multistate/multiregional population projection for India and added two dimensions, the labour force participation and the sector of activity. For fertility, mortality, migration, and education, the input files already include rates for each projected year. Therefore, alternative scenarios can be built simply by changing the value of the inputs.

The parameters for the labour force participation and the sector of activity are however regression parameters. The sector of activity has a "cohort" parameter that allows change over time, but labour force participation does not. Assuming no change in parameters means that change in labour force participation would only result from changes in the composition of the population by age, sex, education, region and fertility (as a reminder, we have a parameter for women who had a kid in the past

---

Electronic supplementary material The online version of this chapter (https://doi.org/10.1007/978-3-030-79111-7_5) contains supplementary material, which is available to authorized users.

© The Author(s) 2021
G. Marois and S. KC, *Microsimulation Population Projections with SAS*, SpringerBriefs in Population Studies,
https://doi.org/10.1007/978-3-030-79111-7_5

5 years). As the model is constructed at this point, changing a parameter in the input file would generate an immediate change starting from 2015, with no further evolution for the rest of the projection.

In this chapter, we will show two examples of alternative scenarios. In the first one, we test a scenario in which women with a young child at home would have the same participation rate and probability of working in the formal sector as other women, all other things being equal. In the second one, we test a scenario in which the labour force participation rates of women gradually increase and reach those of men in 2060. Obviously, none of these scenarios have a predictive purpose. They should be interpreted as "what if" scenarios that aim to measure how the model reacts to change in its different components and provide some policy-relevant information about the socioeconomic dynamics of the country.

5.2 Example 1: The Impact of Having a Young Child on Labour Force Participation and the Sector of Activity

For the first example of an alternative scenario, we will test one in which women with a young child at home have the same participation rate and the same chance to work in the formal sector as other women, all other things being equal. When creating an alternative scenario, the first thing to do is to copy and paste the folder where codes, parameters, and outputs are located. Otherwise, files will be replaced. In the example presented above, the folder was called "Chap. 4". We copy and paste this folder and change the name to "In this chapter_YoungChild".

This alternative scenario is easy to create and doesn't require any major change in the codes. We can just switch to 0 the two parameters for young_kid in parameters files lfp.csv and formal.csv that are applied to women with a young kid, as highlighted in yellow in Fig. 5.1.

We then change the name of the scenario in the %let statement. This will automatically change the name of the scenario folder everywhere in the codes.

```
%let scenario_name= Chapter5_YoungChild;
```

We can then run the scenario and explore the results in the file outputTotal.csv. In Fig. 5.2, we compare the projected labour force size for women from this scenario to the Chap. 4 scenario. For the purpose of this analysis, we will consider Chap. 4 scenario as the "reference" scenario, since it is the business as usual scenario with constant parameters. In 2060, the scenario YoungChild manages to increase the number of female workers by 6%, by switching 7 million housewives into workers. This scenario also increases the number of women working in the formal sector by 6 M, an increase of 10% compared to the reference scenario.

Indeed, as shown in Fig. 5.3, the scenario YoungChild manages to improve the participation rate as well as the proportion of workers in the formal sector by several

5.2 Example 1: The Impact of Having a Young Child on Labour Force … 73

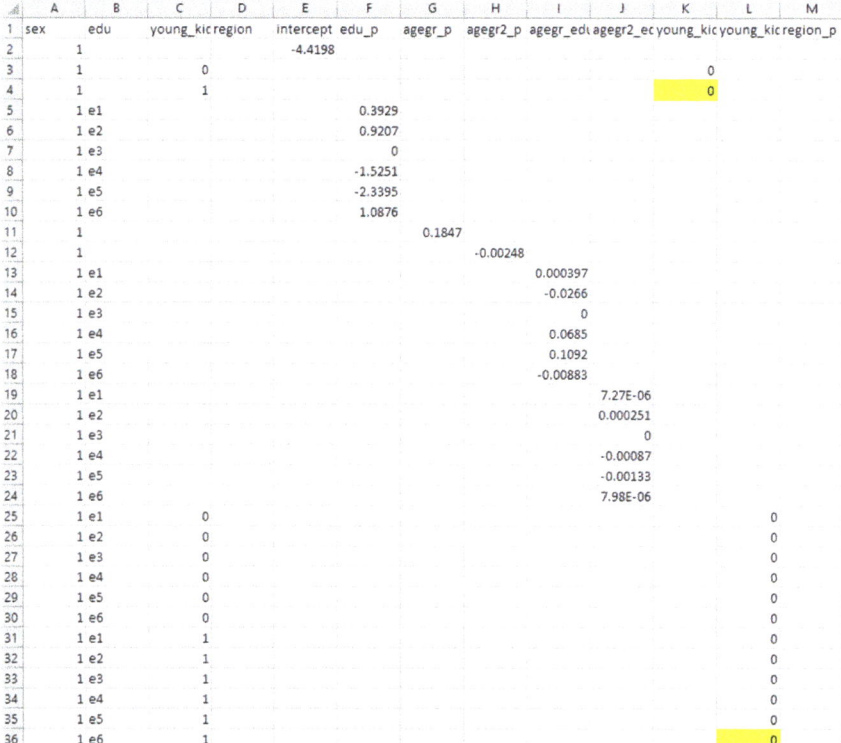

Fig. 5.1 Screenshot of the parameter file lfp.csv for the YoungChild scenario (opened with Excel)

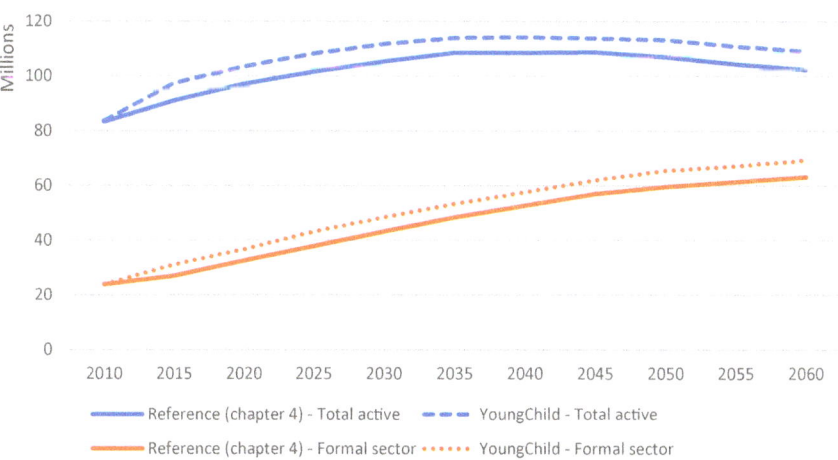

Fig. 5.2 Projected female labour force size in India, 2010–2060, Reference and YoungChild scenarios

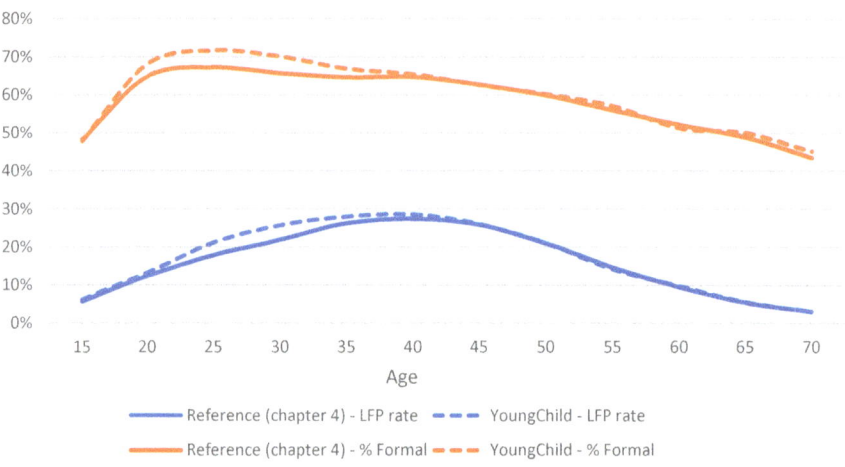

Fig. 5.3 Projected labour force participation rate and proportion of workers in the formal sector by age in 2060, women, India, Reference and YoungChild scenarios

percent for the age groups 20 to 34, which are the main age groups that parameters for having a young kid are concerned with. For the labour force participation, this gain is significant, but rates are still way below those of men. This suggests that while having a young kid at home negatively affects the participation rates of women, it is only a minor factor for explaining their lower rates, and policies that seek to change this might focus on other issues.

5.3 Example 2: Gender Equality in Labour Force Participation

In this second example of an alternative scenario (GenderEquality), we test a scenario in which labour force participation rates of women gradually increase and reach those of men (with the same age/education/region) by 2060. This scenario will show the impact on the labour force of an efficient policy reducing gender equalities and empowering women. For this kind of scenario, where changes occur gradually over time, we cannot directly change the parameter for women in the input parameters file lfp.csv because this would generate an immediate change in the labour force participation.

We will show in this section how to adapt the model to make changes in parameters gradually over a period of years. We will build a scenario in which parameters for women reach those of men by 2060 (though keeping the negative parameters for having a young child). As there are no big gaps between men and women for the proportion of workers in the formal sector, we will not touch this module.

5.3 Example 2: Gender Equality in Labour Force Participation

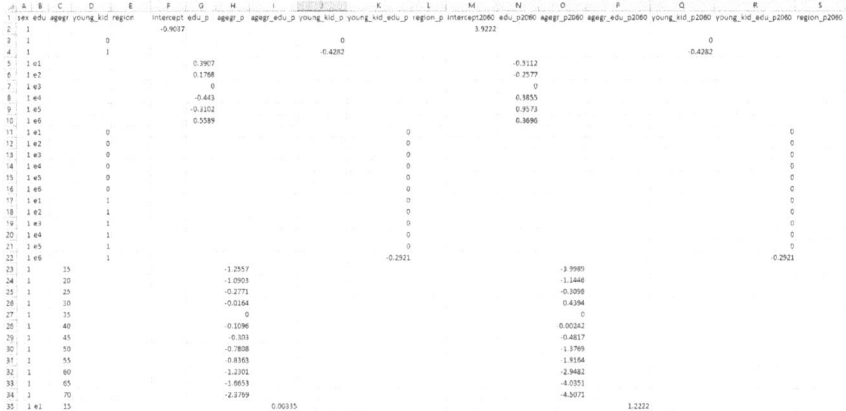

Fig. 5.4 Screenshot of the parameter file lfp.csv for the scenario GenderEquality (opened with Excel)

Since this is a new scenario, we again need to copy and paste the model and its assumptions for reference (Chap. 4) into a new folder (we label it "In this chapter_GenderEquality"). In the code, we then change the name of the scenario accordingly:

```
%let scenario_name= Chapter5_GenderEquality;
```

We then need to reshape the input file for labour force participation. For women, we have initial parameters for 2015, and we want those parameters to gradually evolve until they reach those of men in 2060. The parameter file thus needs to have two columns for each set of parameters: one for the initial value, one for the value of 2060. In Fig. 5.4, we show how the file should look. Columns A to E are variable names and their categories. Columns F to L are their corresponding initial parameters. Columns M to S (ending in "2060") are their corresponding parameters in 2060, which are a copy of the men's parameters (plus the parameters for the variable young_kid and its interaction with education).

We merge this parameter file to the population file in the labour force module in a way similar to what we did previously, with SQL codes. From the code for Chapter 4, we simply add for each variable of the model the name of parameters in 2060 from the input file, as highlighted in yellow in the code below.

```sas
/*Labor force participation*/
/*Implementing parameters*/
   proc sql;
     create table pop_lfp1 as
       select
         p.*,
         t1.intercept, t1.intercept2060, t2.edu_p, t2.edu_p2060,
  t3.agegr_p, t3.agegr_p2060,t4.agegr2_p, t4.agegr2_p2060, t5.agegr_edu_p,
  t5.agegr_edu_p2060,t6.agegr2_edu_p, t6.agegr2_edu_p2060, t7.young_kid_p,
  t7.young_kid_p2060,t8.young_kid_edu_p, t8.young_kid_edu_p2060, t9.region_p
         , t9.region_p2060
       from
         pop2 p
         left join
         ( select sex, intercept, intercept2060
           from param.lfp
           where not missing(intercept)
         ) t1
         on p.sex=t1.sex
         left join
         ( select sex, edu, edu_p, edu_p2060
           from param.lfp
           where not missing(edu_p)
         )t2
         on p.sex=t2.sex and p.edu=t2.edu
         left join
         ( select sex, agegr_p, agegr_p2060
           from param.lfp
           where not missing(agegr_p)
         )t3
         on p.sex=t3.sex
         left join
         ( select sex, agegr2_p, agegr2_p2060
           from param.lfp
           where not missing(agegr2_p)
         )t4
         on p.sex=t4.sex
         left join
         ( select sex, edu, agegr_edu_p, agegr_edu_p2060
           from param.lfp
           where not missing(agegr_edu_p)
         )t5
         on p.sex=t5.sex and p.edu=t5.edu
         left join
         ( select sex, edu, agegr2_edu_p, agegr2_edu_p2060
           from param.lfp
           where not missing(agegr2_edu_p)
         )t6
         on p.sex=t6.sex and p.edu=t6.edu
         left join
         ( select sex, young_kid, young_kid_p, young_kid_p2060
           from param.lfp
           where not missing(young_kid_p)
         )t7
         on p.sex=t7.sex and p.young_kid=t7.young_kid
         left join
         ( select sex, edu, young_kid, young_kid_edu_p, young_kid_edu_p2060
           from param.lfp
           where not missing(young_kid_edu_p)
         )t8
         on p.sex=t8.sex and p.edu=t8.edu and p.young_kid=t8.young_kid
         left join
          ( select sex, region, region_p, region_p2060
           from param.lfp
           where not missing(region_p)
          )t9
         on p.sex=t9.sex and p.region=t9.region;
   quit;
```

5.3 Example 2: Gender Equality in Labour Force Participation

In the resulting population file pop_lfp1, each individual has logit parameters for the year 2010 and 2060. We now need to adjust the calculation of the labour force participation rate in the section simulating the labour force participation event in the temporary population file pop_lfp2 for the population aged 15–74.

```
/*Labour force participation event*/
data work.pop_lfp2;
set work.pop_lfp1;
labour=0;
if 15<=agegr<74 then do;
(…)
```

In the temporary variables *lab2010* and *lab2060*, we sum up those parameters for the initial (2010) and final (2060) years, respectively.

```
    (…)
    lab2010 = intercept + agegr_p*agegr + agegr2_p*agegr*agegr + edu_p +
agegr_edu_p*agegr + agegr2_edu_p*agegr*agegr
    + region_p + young_kid_p + young_kid_edu_p;
    lab2060 = intercept2060 + agegr_p2060*agegr + agegr2_p2060*agegr*agegr +
edu_p2060 + agegr_edu_p2060*agegr + agegr2_edu_p2060*agegr*agegr
    + region_p2060 + young_kid_p2060 + young_kid_edu_p2060;
    (…)
```

Then, in another temporary variable *lab*, we interpolate the sum of logit parameters for the current period (endyr). From this, we calculate the corresponding probability of participating in the labour force (*prob_lab*) and simulate the event with a random experiment.

```
(…)
lab = lab2010 + (&endyr-2010)*(lab2060 - lab2010) /(2060-2010);
prob_lab=exp(lab)/(1+exp(lab));
if rand('uniform')<prob_lab then labour=1;
end;
(…)
```

Finally, we drop parameters and temporary variables.

```
    ( )
    drop intercept agegr_p agegr2_p edu_p agegr_edu_p agegr2_edu_p region_p young_kid_p
young_kid_edu_p lab prob_lab lab2010 lab2060
    intercept2060 agegr_p2060 agegr2_p2060 edu_p2060 agegr_edu_p2060 agegr2_edu_p2060
region_p2060 young_kid_p2060 young_kid_edu_p2060;
    run;
```

No further changes are required to run this scenario. The interpolation implemented directly in the code of the model allows for a smooth and gradual increase of the labour force participation rates of women, as shown in Fig. 5.5 which has been built from the file outputTotal.csv.

Results of this scenario would give approximatively the same population size by age, sex, education and region as the reference scenario in Chap. 4, but very different outcomes in terms of labour force size, as shown in Fig. 5.6. The size of the workforce is thus about 60% higher in the GenderEquality scenario than in the baseline scenario (1.0G vs. 0.6G), and therefore, the country reaps a much greater benefit from the demographic dividend, as suggested by the labour force dependency ratio which, by 2060 in the GenderEquality scenario, is less than half of what it was in the reference scenario (0.79 versus 1.86). This outcome highlights the high stakes of including labour force participation and its sources of heterogeneity in population projections.

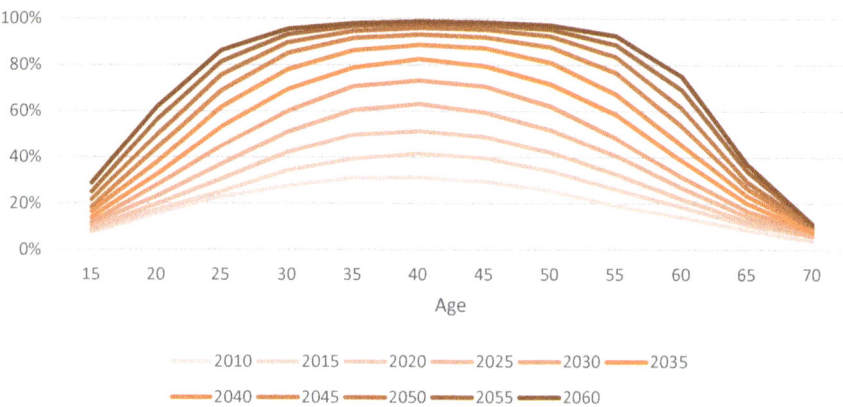

Fig. 5.5 Projected labour force participation rates by age for women, India, 2010–2060, GenderEquality scenario

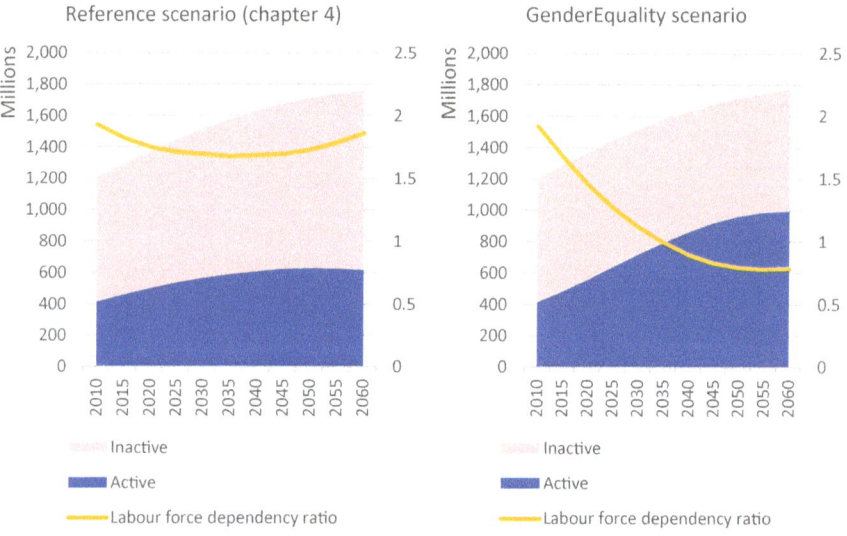

Fig. 5.6 Projected population according to the labour force status, India, 2010–2060, Reference and GenderEquality scenarios

Open Access This chapter is licensed under the terms of the Creative Commons Attribution 4.0 International License (http://creativecommons.org/licenses/by/4.0/), which permits use, sharing, adaptation, distribution and reproduction in any medium or format, as long as you give appropriate credit to the original author(s) and the source, provide a link to the Creative Commons license and indicate if changes were made.

The images or other third party material in this chapter are included in the chapter's Creative Commons license, unless indicated otherwise in a credit line to the material. If material is not included in the chapter's Creative Commons license and your intended use is not permitted by statutory regulation or exceeds the permitted use, you will need to obtain permission directly from the copyright holder.

Chapter 6
Extending and Adapting the Model

Abstract This chapter shows different ways of extending or adapting the model built in previous chapters for other contexts. We show how adding and removing modules, how changing the country, how implementing a deterministic approach for some events and how calibrating projection outcomes on other projections.

Keywords Microsimulation · Population projection · Demography · Method · SAS

6.1 A Flexible Model

In previous chapters, we translated a multistate model projecting education in India and its regions into a microsimulation model, then added two new dimensions, labour force participation and sector of activity, for which we showed examples of alternative scenarios.

The framework of the model can be easily adapted for other purposes. Adapting it for another country would only require us to change the population and parameters files accordingly, while changes in the code would be minor, such as changing the name of regions in the migration module, or if the number of categories of education is different, adapting the code to a larger or smaller number of categories accordingly. Depending on our needs, we could also change the modelling of certain events or add events.

In this chapter, we will adapt the model for another projection with different attributes. We will replicate the multistate projection for China from the Wittgenstein Center (Lutz et al. 2018); we will add labour force participation, and we will calibrate the outcomes on the medium variant of the World Population Prospects (United

---

Electronic supplementary material The online version of this chapter (https://doi.org/10.1007/978-3-030-79111-7_6) contains supplementary material, which is available to authorized users.

Nations 2019). Compared to the projection for India we built in Chaps. 3 and 4, this projection model has the following differences:

- It is not multiregional. We need therefore to turn off the domestic migration module and the shift from rural to urban areas;
- The projection is not closed, which means there is international migration;
- The time span is 2015 to 2100.

In this section, we will detail the required changes in the microsimulation model, beginning by naming the scenario. All changes made compare to the code from Chap. 4 are highlighted in yellow.

```
%let scenario_name=Chapter6_China;
```

6.2 Updating Input Files

Before making further changes in the code, input files need to be updated, including the base population and parameters files. The simulation needs to start from a new micro dataset that matches the population of China in 2015 by age, sex and education. We created this new base population with the exact same procedure as in Chap. 2, but using a different input for the aggregated population (taken from Lutz et al. (2018)). The base population, POP_2015.csv is created in the folder Chapter6_China/Population. The code and the input file can be found in the folder Chapter6_China/NewBasePop. Although we only build an example for China in this section, Lutz et al. (2018) provide data with a similar structure for all countries of the world.

Updated parameters are provided in the folder "Chapter6_China/Parameters". For the demographic and education dimensions, parameters are extracted from the SSP2 scenario of Lutz et al. (2018). Because the projection is not multiregional, there are no files for domestic migration (dom_mig), rural to urban shifts (ur), or for the sector of activity (formal and formal_input), as these dimensions are not included in this adaptation of the model. The structure of other parameter files stays the same and updated parameters can be directly implemented in files. The region variable is also useless, as there is only one region. However, it's better to keep it in the input file and fill it in with a single value, such as "China", as illustrated in Fig. 6.1 showing an example for the parameter file fertility.csv. Otherwise, an additional change would be required in the microsimulation code.

For the parameter file for the labour force participation module (lfp_.csv) and for the imputation of labour force participation in the base population (lfp_imput.csv), we used pooled data of waves 2010 to 2017 of the Chinese General Social Survey (CGSS) to re-estimate the logistic regression model predicting the labour force with personal characteristics (see Eq. 4.1 from the labour force participation module presented in Chap. 4). However, the education variable in the CGSS has only 5 categories: no

6.2 Updating Input Files

	A	B	C	D	E	F
1	region	sex	aeggr	edu	year	asfr
2	China	1	15	e1	2015	0.018111
3	China	1	15	e2	2015	0.018111
4	China	1	15	e3	2015	0.016639
5	China	1	15	e4	2015	0.009544
6	China	1	15	e5	2015	9.90E-07
7	China	1	15	e6	2015	9.90E-07
8	China	1	20	e1	2015	0.174476
9	China	1	20	e2	2015	0.174476
10	China	1	20	e3	2015	0.160288
11	China	1	20	e4	2015	0.13555
12	China	1	20	e5	2015	0.076428
13	China	1	20	e6	2015	0.021548
14	China	1	25	e1	2015	0.130338

Fig. 6.1 Screenshot of the parameter file "fertility.csv" (opened with excel)

education, primary completed, lower secondary, upper secondary and postsecondary. Therefore, in the regression model, the category "no education" includes incomplete primary. The parameters are implemented accordingly in the parameter files.

The statistical model also doesn't include the region, because the projection is not multistate, nor the presence of children at home, because this survey is not suitable for the inclusion of this variable. Therefore, in the parameter files, the variable for the presence of a young kid at home (young_kid_p) and its interaction with education (young_kid_edu_p) are set to 0 (see Fig. 6.2, which highlights in yellow parameters that are switched to 0). Similarly, the number of categories for the variable "region" is reduced to only one, which is set to "China" and also takes the value 0. Adapting the parameter file in such a way, that is, setting to 0 parameters of variables that are not used in the modelling rather than removing them from the file, allows us to minimize changes in the code of the labour force participation module.

Other parameters are implemented from regression models. As compared to India, gender gaps are much less prominent in China, as rates of labour force participation for women are only 10 to 15% lower than those of men (see Fig. 6.3). Chinese women with postsecondary education indeed already have rates that are close to those of men. The gender gap exists mainly for individuals with lower education. For both males and females, rates are lower for the populations with no education or primary education for most of adulthood, but become higher past the age of 60, implying that retirement comes later for the minimally educated population.

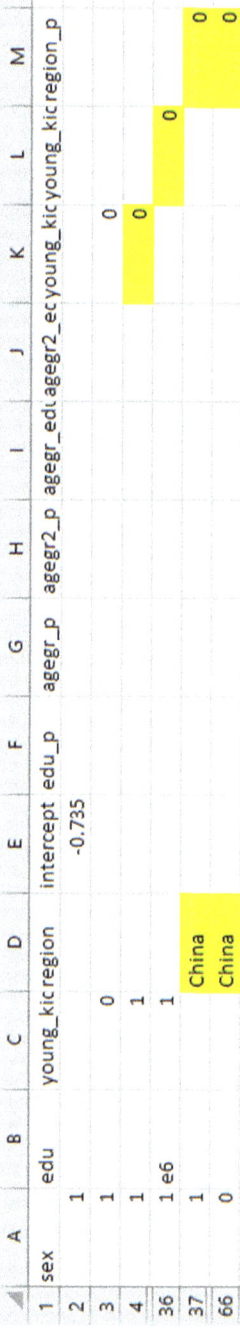

Fig. 6.2 Screenshot of the parameter file lfp.csv (opened with excel)

6.3 Changing the Time Span of the Projection

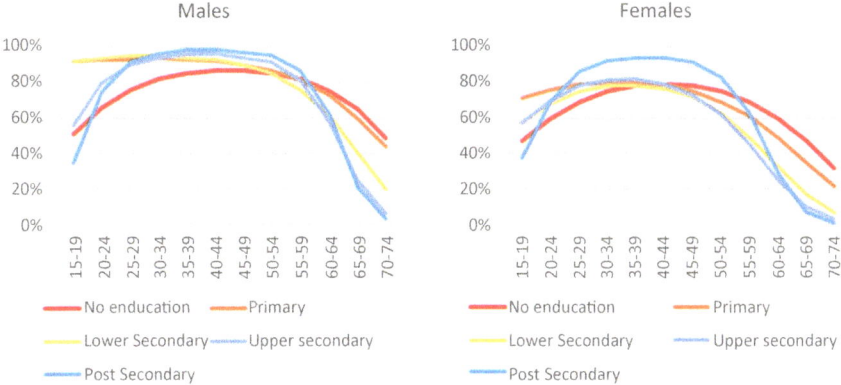

Fig. 6.3 Predicted labour force participation rate by age, sex and education, China. *Source* National Sample Survey on Employment and Unemployment 2017/2018 (India); Chinese General Social Survey 2010–2015 (China)

6.3 Changing the Time Span of the Projection

The time span of this projection is 2015 to 2100 instead of 2010 to 2060. The base population is now pop_2015.csv in the population folder. We thus change the code to import accordingly:

```
%import
("C:\Users\Guillaume\Desktop\Microsimulation\&scenario_name\Population\
POP_2015.csv",pop.pop_2015);
```

The first thing to do is change the value in the macro loop, calling the simulation accordingly. (As a reminder, the second parameter corresponds to the starting year of the last loop. Thus, 2095 implies that the last loop simulates 2095 to 2100).

```
%loop(2015, 2095);
```

Then, we need to adjust the code in the imputation of the base population section in order to select the proper file, which is pop_2015 instead of pop_2010.

```
/*Imputing the labour force participation and the sector of activity for 2015*/
   /*Labour force participation*/
   /*Implementing parameters*/

      proc sql;
         create table work.lfp_imput as
           select
             p.*,
             t1.intercept, t2.edu_p, t3.agegr_p, t4.agegr2_p, t5.agegr_edu_p,
             t6.agegr2_edu_p,t7.region_p
           from
             pop.pop_2015 p
             (...)
```

Then, in the count of the population, we set the proper year (2015 instead of 2010) in the label for the output files.

```
/*Population by age, sex, region, education, and lfp for 2015*/
proc freq data=work.lfp_imput2 noprint;
table  year*agegr*sex*edu*region*formal/list norow nocol nopercent nocum
out=work.output2015(rename=(count=pop) drop=percent);
weight weight;
run;

proc transpose data=work.output2015 out=work.output2015(rename=(_0=inactive _1=Informal
_2=Formal) drop=_name_ _label_);
var pop;
by year agegr sex edu region;
id formal;
run;

data results.output2015;
set work.output2015;
(…)
run;
```

6.4 Turning Off Modules

There are different ways to turn off a module. If we want to minimize change in the code, we might simply switch values in the parameters files of those modules to 0. Doing so, the event will still be simulated, but since all probabilities are 0, the event will never occur. This is the simpler option, but it has the inconvenience of loading the model with unnecessary calculations, which increases the running time of the simulation. If the sample is large, depending on the power of the computer, this might generate significant unnecessary delay. In the following example, we will show how to turn off the code of the module in order to remove unnecessary calculations from the simulation.

The first thing to do is to remove code lines importing the parameters files of those modules. Because there is no domestic migration, no rural to urban shifts and no sector of activity, the code lines importing parameters (dom_mig.csv, ur.csv, formal.csv and formal_input.csv) should not be read anymore. This can be done either simply by erasing the code, or, as we do in the code below, by embedding it between /*…*/. This latter method allows to keep the code without reading it (the color is then changed to green) and can be useful if we want to reactive these codes later.

6.4 Turning Off Modules

```
(...)
/*%import
("C:\Users\Guillaume\Desktop\Microsimulation\&scenario_name\parameters\
dom_mig.csv",param.dom_mig);*/
/*%import
("C:\Users\Guillaume\Desktop\Microsimulation\scenario_name\parameters\
ur.csv",param.ur);*/%import
("C:\Users\Guillaume\Desktop\Microsimulation\&scenario_name\parameters\
lfp.csv",param.lfp); /*%import
("C:\Users\Guillaume\Desktop\Microsimulation\scenario_name\parameters\
formal.csv",param.formal);*/
%import ("C
C:\Users\Guillaume\Desktop\Microsimulation\&scenario_name\parameters\
lfp_imput.csv",param.lfp_imput);
/*%import
("C:\Users\Guillaume\Desktop\Microsimulation\&scenario_name\parameters\
formal_imput.csv",param.formal_imput);*/
(...)
```

We also do the same for the code sorting these files.

```
/*proc sort data=param.dom_mig; by region agegr edu sex;run;*/
/*proc sort data=param.ur; by region;run;*/
```

6.4.1 Domestic Migration and Rural to Urban Reclassification

The model for China is multistate, but not multiregional. Therefore, we need to switch off the domestic migration and the rural to urban shifts modules and, consequently, adjust the outputs. Again, we simply embed the code in /*…*/.

```
/*Domestic migration module*/
    /*proc sort data=work.pop_edu; by region agegr edu sex;run;
    data work.pop_dm;
    merge work.pop_edu(in=in1) param.dom_mig;
    by region agegr edu sex;
    if in1;

(...)

    drop i a AN_urban--WB_rural a newregion;
    run;*/
```

Because this code is not read anymore, the population file "pop_dm" is not created. We therefore need to change the population file read in the next module accordingly, in our case, the fertility module. The fertility module thus needs to start from the last population file created, which is now "pop_edu" rather than "pop_dm".

```
/*Fertility module*/
    /*Adjusting age for exposure*/
    data work.pop_birth;
    set work.pop_edu;
    (...)
```

We then embed similarly the reclassification of rural to urban areas module in order to switch it off.

```
/*Reclassification of rural to urban areas*/
/*proc sort data=work.pop_birth3; by region; run;
data work.pop_reclass;
merge work.pop_birth3 (in=in1) param.ur;
by region;
if in1;

oldregion2=region;
if death=0 and substr(region,4,5)='rural' then do;
    if rand('uniform')<ur then do;
    region=tranwrd(region,'rural','urban');
    reclass=1; end;
end;

drop ur;
run;*/
```

Again, because the temporary population file "pop_reclass" is not created anymore, we modify the starting population file of the next module (updating the characteristics) with the last one ("pop_birth3").

```
/*Time module - Updating characteristics*/
data work.pop2;
set work.pop_birth3;
(…)
```

The fertility module used the variable "region_fert", which was created in the domestic mobility so that the fertility risk would have the right exposure. Since the module is deactivated, the variable is not created and is not useful anymore. Indeed, the region of the mother cannot change during the period. Therefore, the region in which she gives birth does not need to be tracked anymore. However, replacing it everywhere it was used with the variable "region" would be more complicated than simply creating elsewhere a new variable "region_fert" that is a duplicate of region. We add this line at the beginning of the fertility module, in the section adjusting age for exposure.

```
/*Fertility module*/
    /*Adjusting age for exposure and recreating the variable region_fert*/
    data work.pop_birth;
    set work.pop_edu;
    agegr_fert=agegr;
    if rand('uniform')<0.5 then agegr_fert=agegr+5;
    region_fert=region;
    run;
```

Also, in the fertility module, newborns had the possibility of domestic migration, which was assessed by comparing the region of birth and the region of residence at the end of the period. We need to remove this line of code.

6.4 Turning Off Modules

```
/*Fertility module*/
(...)
    /*Create newborn and set their characteristics*/
    output;
    if young_kid=1 then do;
        birth=1;
        age_moth=agegr_fert;
        agegr=-5; young_kid=0; death=0; cohort=year; region_birth=region_fert;
        /*dom_mig=0; if region_birth ne region then dom_mig=1;*/
        sex=0; if rand('uniform')<(srb/(srb+1000)) then sex=1;
        eduM=edu_fert;
        edu='e1';
        if 5*asfr>1 then weight=weight*5*asfr;
        output;
    end;
run;
```

We then need to withdraw the count of domestic migration and rural reclassification in the section generating the outputs. For this purpose, again we simply embed the corresponding code between /*…*/.

```
/*Components of population growth*/
    (...)
    /*proc freq data=work.pop2 noprint;
    table year*agegr*sex*edu*region/list norow nocol nopercent nocum
out=work.inflow(rename=(count=inflow) drop=percent);
    weight weight;
    where dom_mig=1 and death=0;
    run;

    proc freq data=work.pop2 noprint;
    table year*agegr*sex*edu*oldregion/list norow nocol nopercent nocum
out=work.outflow(rename=(count=outflow oldregion=region) drop=percent);
    weight weight;
    where dom_mig=1 and death=0;
    run;

    proc freq data=work.pop2 noprint;
    table year*agegr*sex*edu*region/list norow nocol nopercent nocum
out=work.gain_urban(rename=(count=gain_urban) drop=percent);
    weight weight;
    where reclass=1 and dom_mig ne 1 and death=0;
    run;

    proc freq data=work.pop2 noprint;
    table year*agegr*sex*edu*oldregion2/list norow nocol nopercent nocum
out=work.loss_rural(rename=(count=loss_rural oldregion2=region) drop=percent);
    weight weight;
    where reclass=1 and dom_mig ne 1 and death=0;
    run;*/
    (...)
```

The section cleaning the population file for the next period removes temporary variables created to track demographic events. As there is no more domestic mobility and no rural to urban transitions, variables tracking those events need to be removed from the code.

```
/*Cleaning the population file for next period*/
data pop.pop_&endyr;
set work.pop_lfp2;

if death=1 then delete;
drop birth /*dom_mig reclass oldregion oldregion2*/ region_birth;
run;
```

Finally, in the section merging the population count to the components of growth, we remove datasets for the count of these removed components, inflow, outflow, gain_urban and loss_rural.

```
/*Merging the population count and components of growth*/
(...)
data results.output&endyr;
merge work.outputpop work.birth work.death /*work.inflow work.outflow
work.gain_urban work.loss_rural*/;
by year agegr sex edu region;
(...)
```

6.4.2 Sector of Activity

The model for China we are building also does not include the sector of activity. We thus switch off the module in a similar way. However, this needs to be done twice, because the module includes a subtitle ("Formal–Informal event") that is also embedded in /*…*/.

```
/*Sector of activity*/
    /*Implementing parameters*/
    /*proc sql;
      create table pop_formal1 as
        select
          p.*,
          t1.intercept, t2.edu_p, t3.cohort_p, t4.cohort_region_p,
          t5.young_kid_p, t6.young_kid_edu_p, t7.region_p
(...)
        left join
        ( select sex, region, region_p
          from param.formal
          where not missing(region_p)
        )t7
        on p.sex=t7.sex and p.region=t7.region;
    quit;*/

    /*Formal - Informal event*/
    /*data work.pop_formal2;
    set work.pop_formal1;
(...)
    drop intercept cohort_p edu_p cohort_region_p region_p young_kid_p young_kid_edu_p
exp_form prob_form cohort2;
    run;*/
```

Since the population file formal2 is not created anymore, we then change the starting population file in the next step to make it correspond to the last one created, pop_lfp2.

6.4 Turning Off Modules

```
/*Cleaning the population file for next period*/
data pop.pop_&endyr;
set work.pop_lfp2;
(…)
```

The section generating outputs also needs to be adjusted. As a reminder, the variable "formal" was used to calculate the active population by adding those working in the formal sector to those working in the informal one. In the code producing the population count output, we replace the variable "formal" with the variable "labour" and label categories accordingly (changes highlighted in yellow).

```
/*Generating outputs*/
    /*Population by age sex region education, and lfp*/
    proc freq data=pop.pop_&endyr noprint;
    table   year*agegr*sex*edu*region*labour/list norow nocol nopercent nocum
out=work.outputpop(rename=(count=pop) drop=percent);
    weight weight;
    run;

    proc transpose data=work.outputpop out=work.outputpop(rename=(
(_0=inactive _1=active) drop=_name_ _label_);
    var pop;
    by year agegr sex edu region;
    id labour;
    run;
```

Finally, in the section merging the population count and components of growth, the calculation of the active population from the variables "formal" and "informal" can be removed, as this variable is already included in the dataset.

```
    /*Merging the population count and components of growth*/
    (…)
    data results.output&endyr;
    merge work.outputpop work.birth work.death /*work.inflow work.outflow
work.gain_urban work.loss_rural*/;
    by year agegr sex edu region;
    (…)

    /*active=formal+informal;*/
    pop=inactive+active;
    run;
```

The simulation can then be run. However, we need to adjust in similar way the section imputing the base population. We embed the code for the imputation of the sector of activity in /*…*/, since this variable is not projected.

```
/*Sector of activity*/
 /*Implementing parameters*/
 /*proc sql;
   create table work.formal_imput as
     select
       p.*,
       t1.intercept, t2.edu_p, t3.cohort_p, t4.cohort_region_p,
       t5.region_p

   (...)
     on p.sex=t5.sex and p.region=t5.region;
 quit;
 */
 /*Formal - Informal imputation*/
 /*data work.formal_imput2;
 set work.formal_imput;
 (...)

 drop intercept cohort_p edu_p cohort_region_p region_p exp_form prob_form cohort2;
 run;*/
```

Then, in the population count, we change the variable "formal" to the variable "labour" and set the appropriate labels for categories.

```
/*Population by age, sex, region, education, and lfp for 2015*/
proc freq data=work.lfp_imput2 noprint;
table  year*agegr*sex*edu*region*labour/list norow nocol nopercent nocum
out=work.output2015(rename=(count=pop) drop=percent);
weight weight;
run;


proc transpose data=work.output2015 out=work.output2015(rename=
(_0=inactive _1=active) drop=_name_ _label_);
var pop;
by year agegr sex edu region;
id labour;
run;
```

Finally, we remove the code calculating the variable "active" from the variables "formal" and informal".

```
data results.output2015;
set work.output2015;
(...)
/*active=formal+informal;*/
pop=inactive+active;

run;
```

6.5 Building a Deterministic Module in a Microsimulation Model for International Migration

All events in the modules we have shown so far have been modelled stochastically, with random experiments. For some modules, however, we may want to use a deterministic approach. This could be appropriate if we want to perfectly calibrate an event in a multistate cohort-component projection, or if the sample size for some

6.5 Building a Deterministic Module in a Microsimulation Model ...

subgroups of interest is too small (as there is no Monte Carlo error in the deterministic approach). A microsimulation model can incorporate this kind of modelling. We will show how to model an event deterministically, using international migration as an example.

In the examples we presented in Chaps. 3, 4 and 5, the population was closed: KC et al. (2018) assumed no international migration. However, other scenarios or projections might require the implementation of international migration modules. In this example, international migration is implemented through two new modules, emigration and immigration, which are modelled independently. In the projections of Lutz et al. (2018) that we replicate, international migration is implemented after mortality and education events, but before fertility. International immigrants are therefore not in the population that is at risk of dying or changing their level of education in the period in which they arrive, but they can have children.

Although the deterministic approach has the advantage of having no Monte Carlo error, and though it works quite well for events such as mortality and international migration, it can be very complex for other events, such as fertility. It requires the duplication of all women of reproductive age and the consequent adjustment of the weight of the new births, based on the fertility rate. In doing so, the number of rows in the dataset quickly becomes very large (all women aged 15–49 are duplicated in each step). The same issue occurs for interregional migration.

6.5.1 Emigration

If implemented stochastically, the emigration event can be modelled in the same way as mortality, by simply comparing the emigration rate to a random number, flagging emigrants, and deleting them from the dataset at the beginning of the next period. When implemented deterministically, no observations are deleted: only sample weights change.

The parameters file for the emigration includes emigration rates (emx) by age, sex and education, as shown in Fig. 6.4. For this scenario, emigration rates are thus constant throughout the projection, but this can be changed by simply adding a column "year" to the parameters file.

The international migration event occurs after the education event and is therefore implemented right after the education module. It starts from the temporary population file pop_edu. We merge the parameter file param.emig to the population file pop_edu in the same way we did for events modelled with a stochastic approach.

```
/*Emigration module - Deterministic*/
    proc sort data=work.pop_edu; by agegr edu sex; run;
    data work.pop_emig;
    merge work.pop_edu(in=in1)  param.emig;
    by  agegr edu sex;
    if in1;
    (...)
```

	A	B	C	D
1	sex	agegr	edu	emx
2	0	0	e1	0.000238
3	1	0	e1	0.000238
4	0	5	e1	0.000349
5	1	5	e1	0.000344
6	0	10	e1	0.000487
7	1	10	e1	0.000461
8	0	15	e1	0.000666
9	1	15	e1	0.000638
10	0	20	e1	0.000865
11	1	20	e1	0.000879

Fig. 6.4 Screenshot of the parameters file emig.csv (opened with excel)

In the deterministic approach, the number of people who don't emigrate is determined by adjusting weights according to emigration rates. We store the weight at time t in a temporary variable "old_weight". For those who survived the mortality module (death = 0), the new weight at time t + 5 (we attribute a new value to variable "weight") is then calculated by multiplying the weight at time t (old_weight) by 1— emigration rate (emx). In a temporary variable "nb_emig", we calculate the difference between weights at time t and t + 5 (old_weight-weight). When we generate outputs, the sum of this variable will give the number of emigrants for the period.

```
(…)
old_weight=weight;
if death=0 then weight=old_weight*(1-emx);
nb_emig=old_weight-weight;

drop emx;
run;
```

6.5.2 Immigration

The international immigration module doesn't require any statistical calculation. Immigrants are simply implemented by merging an immigration microdata file to the population file of the period. This immigration file should have exactly the same structure as the population file. However, we need to set assumptions for the number

6.5 Building a Deterministic Module in a Microsimulation Model …

and composition of the immigrants. For this, we use the aggregated number of immigrants in China by age, sex, education and year, taken from Lutz et al. (2018), which are generated from international migration flows, taking into account changes in the composition of the world population. From this file, we create the immigration microdata file using the same code as the one used to create the base population (see Chap. 2), but we add a variable "immig = 1" to keep track of immigrants. The output CSV file is labelled "immig.csv" and is stored in the subfolder "parameter". The complete code and the aggregated CSV file can be found in the subfolder "ImmigrationFile" of this chapter.

The immigration file, from which we select only immigrants of the period (year = &styr), can then be concatenated to the population file of the projection, right after the emigration module in our example.

```
/*Immigration module*/
  data work.pop_immig;
  set work.pop_emig param.immig(where=(year=&styr));
  run;
```

Since we implanted new modules in the middle of the simulation, we need to change the population file on which the next module (fertility) is built, which is now pop_immig instead of pop_edu.

```
/*Fertility module*/
   /*Adjusting age for exposure*/
   data work.pop_birth;
   set work.pop_immig;
   (…)
```

Finally, in the assumptions taken from Lutz et al. (2018), the age of immigrants is their age at the end of the period. We therefore need to exclude immigrants of the period (if immig ne 1) when we increment age in the time module.

```
/*Time module - Updating characteristics*/
data work.pop2;
set work.pop_birth3;
if immig ne 1 and (death=0 or agegr=-5) then agegr=agegr+5;
if death=1 and agegr ne -5 and rand('uniform')<0.5 then agegr=agegr+5;
year=year+5;
run;
```

6.5.3 Adjusting the Exposure in the Fertility Module

As mentioned previously, the age at immigration is the one at the end of the period. Since migrants are submitted to the fertility event, some of them could give birth before aging. For the rest of the population, "age" corresponds to age of the beginning of the period. We therefore exclude immigrants (if immig ne 1) when determining their age at birth.

```
/*Fertility module*/
    /*Adjusting age for exposure*/
    data work.pop_birth;
    set work.pop_immig;
    agegr_fert=agegr;
    if immig ne 1 and rand('uniform')<0.5 then agegr_fert=agegr+5;
    (...)
```

For immigrants, age at birth could be their age at the beginning of the period. Accordingly, we adjust it randomly for half of them.

```
(...)
if immig = 1 and rand('uniform')<0.5 then agegr_fert=agegr-5;
region_fert=region;
run;
```

Immigrants and emigrants are both exposed to the fertility event for part of the year. Therefore, some other minor changes are required in the code of the fertility module. The variable "immig" included in the immigration file allows us to track immigrants of the period. Assuming they arrive in the middle of the period, we add a condition similar to the one used for deaths that allows only half of immigrants to be exposed to the fertility event.

```
        (...)
        /*Fertility event*/
        young_kid=0;
            if death=0 or (death=1 and rand('uniform')<0.5)
or (immig=1 and rand('uniform')<0.5) then do;
                if rand('uniform')<5*asfr then young_kid=1;*Has a kid age 0-4;
            end;
        (...)
```

For emigrants, however, we don't have a variable tracking them, since they are calculated by weight adjustments. We therefore need to add one line in the section for creating a newborn in order to transfer randomly either the old weight (before emigration) or the new weight (after emigration) of the mother to the baby.

```
(...)
/*Create newborn and set their characteristics*/
output;
if young_kid=1 then do;
    birth=1;
    age_moth=agegr_fert;
    agegr=-5; young_kid=0; death=0;  cohort=year; region_birth=region_fert;
    /*dom_mig=0; if region_birth ne region then dom_mig=1;*/
    sex=0; if rand('uniform')<(srb/(srb+1000)) then sex=1;
    eduM=edu_fert;
    edu='e1';
    if rand('uniform')<0.5 then weight=old_weight;
    if 5*asfr>1 then weight=weight*5*asfr;
    output;
end;
run;
```

6.6 Adjusting Outputs and the Population File for the Next Period

Three temporary variables were used in the new emigration and immigration modules, "old_weight" (which was the weight of individuals before emigration), "nb_emig" (used for compiling the number of emigrants) and "immig" (which tracks immigrants). These variables need to be removed, since for the next period, immigrants should not be counted as new immigrants and should be exposed to the complete risk of fertility. We simply add these three variables to the section for cleaning the population for the next period, next to the other temporary variables to drop.

```
/*Cleaning the population file for next period*/
data pop.pop_&endyr;
set work.pop_lfp2;

if death=1 then delete;
drop birth immig old_weight nb_emig /*dom_mig reclass oldregion oldregion2*/
region_birth;
run;
```

Finally, we want to include immigrants and emigrants when generating outputs of the components of growth. Since immigrants are tracked with the variable "immig", we can use it with a proc freq to sum up the number of immigrants by age, sex and education, as we do for other components such as deaths and births.

```
/*Generating outputs*/
(...)
    /*Components of population growth*/
    proc freq data=work.pop2 noprint;
    table year*age_moth*eduM*region_birth/list norow nocol nopercent nocum
out=work.birth(rename=(count=births age_moth=agegr eduM=edu region_birth=region)
drop=percent);
    weight weight;
    where birth=1;
    run;

    proc freq data=work.pop2 noprint;
    table year*agegr*sex*edu*region/list norow nocol nopercent nocum
out=work.death(rename=(count=deaths) drop=percent);
    weight weight;
    where death=1;
    run;

    proc freq data=work.pop2 noprint;
    table year*agegr*sex*edu*region/list norow nocol nopercent nocum
out=work.immigrants(rename=(count=immigrants) drop=percent);
    weight weight;
    where immig=1;
    run;
```

Emigrants don't have a variable tracking them, since they are computed by weight adjustment. To calculate their total number, we need to sum up the variable nb_emig that was calculated in the emigration module by subtracting the weight at the end of the period from the weight at the beginning of the period. This can be done with the tabulate procedure. The outputs table is stored in a dataset "emigrants". In this dataset, we rename the column counting the sum of emigrants (nb_emig_sum) for "emigrants" and drop the unused variables "_table_", "_page_" and "_type_". The statement "var" is used to identify continuous variables, such as nb_emig, while the statement class identifies the categorical variables (year, agegr, sex, edu and region). The table is then built to have the same structure as other datasets for components: we want the sum of emigrants by year, age, sex, education and region.

```
proc tabulate data=work.pop2 out=work.emigrants(rename=(nb_emig_sum=emigrants)
drop=_table_ _page_ _type_);
var nb_emig;
class year agegr sex edu region;
table year*agegr*sex*edu*region, (sum)*nb_emig;
run;
```

Finally, in the section merging population count and components of growth, we add a dataset for the number of immigrants and emigrants.

```
/*Merging the population count and components of growth*/
(...)
data results.output&endyr;
  merge work.outputpop work.birth work.death work.immigrants work.emigrants
/*work.inflow work.outflow work.gain_urban work.loss_rural*/;
  by year agegr sex edu region;
  (...)
```

6.7 Calibrating Simulation Outcomes

For different reasons, we might want to calibrate the projection outcomes on other projections or estimates, either for a specific year or for the entire time span. For instance, the base population of the model we built for India is for 2010, but since then, more recent population estimates by age and sex have been released. We therefore might want to calibrate our outcomes on the more recent estimates, at some point of the projection, such as 2015 or 2020.

A calibration at the end of each period on the outcome of a simpler cohort-component model can also be performed to make two models comparable, or to facilitate the implementation of broader general assumptions. For instance, since our assumptions in the fertility module are age-, region- (for India), and education-specific fertility rates, the total fertility rate (TFR) of India or China will depend on the composition of population, which itself depends on other demographic components of the projection. In other words, we do not know a priori exactly what the forecasted TFR will be, as we do in a cohort-component model. When calibrating on such a model, the underlying assumptions should not be interpreted in terms of their absolute values, but rather in terms of the differences among subgroups.

As example of this calibration, we will calibrate in this section our microsimulation projections of India and China on the projection outcomes of the medium variant scenario of the World Population Prospects (United Nations, 2019) by age, sex and

6.7 Calibrating Simulation Outcomes

year. Doing this will increase the consistency between the demographic assumptions, as they will come from the same source, and this will therefore make their outcomes more comparable. Table 6.1 summarizes the broad assumptions.

For India, demographic assumptions for the whole country are about the same in both projections. The main difference between the two projections is the inclusion of the education and sub-regions dimensions in KC et al. (2018). The difference in the net migration assumptions has a negligible impact on the outcomes, as the numbers (about −500 k per year) are marginal compared to the total population size of the country. Consequently, both projections yield very similar results in terms of age and sex size and composition.

As for China, the difference between the SSP2 scenario of the projection of Lutz et al. (2018) that we used to build the microsimulation model and the medium variant of the World Population Prospects is much more appreciable: the present and future total fertility rates are higher by about 0.3 children per woman in the latter. Detailed explanations concerning the different assumptions for fertility can be found in Basten et al. (2014). Calibrating our microsimulation on those of the World Population Prospects will thus indirectly increase equally the age- and education-specific fertility rates that we took from Lutz et al. (2018) in order to match the number of 0–4 year olds at the end of each period that would be given by a TFR of around 1.7–1.8, as assumed by the World Population Prospects. As the modelling of education is kept as well as differentials in demographic behaviours by educational attainment, the calibration will allow the model to merge the education component of Lutz et al. (2018) and the labour force dimension we added to the official projection of the United Nations.

In this section, we will explain the code for calibration implemented in the model of China. The code calibrating the model of India is however the same and can be found in the file "Chapter 6—India calibrated.sas", located in the folder "Chapter6—India calibrated" in which other files necessary for the projection are also located.

The file calibration.csv, located the subfolder "param", contains the population size by age, sex and year from the World Population Prospects (United Nations, 2019). Figure 6.5 shows an excerpt of the file. The column "pop_wanted" represents the population that will be used for the calibration. At the end of each period, we want our outcomes to match with these. We will proceed by adjusting the individual weights accordingly. Note that the older age group in this file is 100 (for 100+), while in our projection, it goes to 125. We will need to take this into consideration when we will calculate the adjustment factors.

The first thing to do is to import this file and sort it. This is done the same way as we did for all other parameter files, with the macro import and the sort procedure in the section for importing files.

Table 6.1 Summary of demographic assumptions for different projections

	India—World Population Prospects 2019 (medium variant)	India—KC et al. (2018)/uncalibrated microsimulation	China—World Population Prospects 2019 (medium variant)	China—Lutz et al. (2018) (SSP2)/uncalibrated microsimulation
Total fertility rate	2015–2020: 2.24	2015–2020: 2.20	2015–2020: 1.69	2015–2020: 1.44
	2055–2060: 1.76	2055–2060: 1.80	2055–2060: 1.76	2055–2060: 1.41
			2095–2100: 1.77	2095–2100: 1.49
Life expectancy	2015–2020: 69.3	2015–2020: 70.8	2015–2020: 76.6	2015–2020: 76.6
	2055–2060: 76.1	2055–2060: 81.9	2055–2060: 83.0	2055–2060: 83.9
			2095–2100: 87.6	2095–2100: 93.3
Net migration (annual)	2015–2020: −533 K	2015–2020: 0	2015–2020: −348 K	2015–2020: −184 K
	2055–2060: −484 K	2055–2060: 0	2055–2060: −310 K	2055–2060: −148 K
			2095–2100: −310 K	2095–2100: −89 K

6.7 Calibrating Simulation Outcomes

Fig. 6.5 Screenshot of the parameter file calibration.csv (opened with excel)

	A	B	C	D
1	year	sex	agegr	pop_wanted
2	2015	0	0	46437638
3	2015	0	5	45436987
4	2015	0	10	44264668
5	2015	0	15	46554380
6	2015	0	20	51864604
7	2015	0	25	66864149
8	2015	0	30	51711405
9	2015	0	35	49705968
10	2015	0	40	61857540
11	2015	0	45	63435589
12	2015	0	50	51414420
13	2015	0	55	40972684
14	2015	0	60	40173473
15	2015	0	65	25506514
16	2015	0	70	16608422
17	2015	0	75	11127053
18	2015	0	80	5816694
19	2015	0	85	2143736
20	2015	0	90	518059
21	2015	0	95	86423
22	2015	0	100	7600
23	2020	0	0	44456332
24	2020	0	5	46320144
25	2020	0	10	45349923
26	2020	0	15	44103122
27	2020	0	20	46273865

```
%import
("C:\Users\Guillaume\Desktop\Microsimulation\&scenario_name\
parameters\immig.csv",param.immig);
%import
("C:\Users\Guillaume\Desktop\Microsimulation\&scenario_name\
parameters\calibration.csv",param.calibration);
(...)
proc sort data=param.immig; by agegr edu sex year;run;
proc sort data=param.calibration; by year sex agegr;run;
```

The calibration module is implemented directly in the simulation loop, once all demographic events are completed, i.e. between the time module and the labour force participation module. It thus starts from the temporary population file pop2. First, we make the categories of the age group variable match those of the calibration file. All age groups above 100 are thus reassigned to 100, which now includes all of the population aged 100 and above. Before doing this, we store the old age group variable into a temporary variable agegr2 that will be used later.

```
/*Calibration*/
data work.pop2;
set work.pop2;
agegr2=agegr;
if agegr>=100 then agegr=100;
run;
```

Using this redefined age group variable, we then produce an output of the population count by age and sex with the FREQ procedure. We also include the variable "year", since we want the year to appear in the output in order to allow us to match it with the appropriate year of the calibration file. We use the *list* option to have all counts in a single column, and the options *nocol*, *nopercent* and *norow* to remove all percentages from the output. With the *out* option, we store the resulting output table in the work library under the name "simul", from which we drop the column "percent".

```
proc freq data=work.pop2;
table sex*agegr*year/list nocol nopercent norow out=work.simul(drop=percent);
weight weight;
run;
```

The column "count" in the table "work.simul" thus represents the population by age and sex at the end of the period, as simulated without calibration. We now need to calculate the adjustment factor for individual weights. We create the temporary file "factor" by merging work.simul with the calibration file (param.calibration) by year, sex and agegr. As a reminder, in the file param.calibration, the column "pop_wanted" represents the population we want. The adjustment factor is then calculated by dividing pop_wanted by count. So if we simulate 1000 individuals for a specific group, while we want 1100, the adjustment factor is 1.1, meaning that the weights of all individuals in this specific group need to be increased by 10% in order to get the target population. As "pop_wanted" and "count" will not be used anymore, we can drop them with the *drop* statement.

```
data work.factor;
merge work.simul(in=in1) param.calibration;
if in1;
by year sex agegr;
factor=pop_wanted/count;
drop pop_wanted count;
run;
```

We can now adjust the weights in the population file "work.pop2". After sorting it correctly, we merge it by sex and age group with the file "factor" we just created. The variable "weight" can then be adjusted by multiplying it by the variable "factor".

6.7 Calibrating Simulation Outcomes

With the variable agegr2 we created before, we also reassign the detailed age group categories for the population aged 100. Variables "factor" and "agegr2" will not be used after this point and are therefore dropped from the file.

```
proc sort data=work.pop2; by sex agegr; run;
data work.pop2;
merge work.pop2 work.factor;
by sex agegr;
weight=weight*factor;
agegr=agegr2;
drop factor agegr2;
run;
```

The microsimulation now calibrates the population by age and sex on the projections of the World Population Prospects at the end of each period. To get consistent trends in the final outputs, we also need to calibrate the base population. For this purpose, we use the exact same code as described above, but replace the population file "work.pop2" with "pop.pop_2015" (highlighted in yellow). This code is implemented right before the macro simul, after importing and sorting files.

```
/*Calibration of the base population*/
data pop.pop_2015;
set pop.pop_2015;
agegr2=agegr;
if agegr>=100 then agegr=100;
run;

proc freq data=pop.pop_2015;
table sex*agegr*year/list nocol nopercent norow out=work.simul(drop=percent);
weight weight;
run;

data work.factor;
merge work.simul(in=in1) param.calibration;
if in1;
by year sex agegr;
factor=pop_wanted/count;
drop pop_wanted count;
run;

proc sort data=pop.pop_2015; by sex agegr; run;
data pop.pop_2015;
merge pop.pop_2015 work.factor;
by sex agegr;
weight=weight*factor;
agegr=agegr2;
drop factor agegr2;
run;
```

Since the calibration module readjusts the population size by age and sex at every step, the components of demographic growth (births, deaths, migrants, etc.) produced in the outputs are not accurate anymore. Interpretations of these components should thus be made with caution.

6.8 Overview of Results

In Fig. 6.6, we compare the final age pyramid by education from the microsimulation before and after calibration with the one from the medium variant from the World Population Prospects (United Nations, 2019) and from the scenario SSP2 from the multistate model of Lutz et al. (2018). As expected, when not calibrated, demographic components of the microsimulation replicate those of the Lutz et al. (2018) approximately. The total population starts slowly declining in 2025 from 1.4 to 0.8G in 2100. The population is then very old, with modal age groups between 75 and 89, but highly educated, with almost all people of working age having at least an upper secondary education and more than half having postsecondary education.

The calibrated microsimulation yields the same age-sex structure as the World Population Prospects. Both yield a much younger age structure in 2100 and a smaller population, as compared to the non-calibrated scenario (which replicates the demographic growth of Lutz et al. (2018)). These differences are due to the underlying assumptions and not to the modelling. Indeed, the difference is mainly explained by different fertility assumptions. In Lutz et al. (2018), the yearly TFRs range from 1.35 to 1.5 between 2020 and 2100, while they range between 1.7 and 1.8 in the medium variant of the World Population Prospects.

We did a similar calibration for the model of India (see folder Chapter6_India calibrated) in order to make the microsimulation model of India comparable to that of China. In Fig. 6.7, we compare results for China and India. By 2025–2030, India will become the world's largest country in terms of both population size and working-age population (15–64), exceeding China. Both the total and working-age populations will be growing continuously in India, while they will start declining in China. This outcome is well known from other multistate or other cohort-component projections (Lutz et al. 2018; UN 2017). The new outcome of our microsimulation projection model is the labour force participation dimension. We saw in Chap. 4 that India is deprived of many potential workers in its working-age population due to the very low labour force participation of women, while gender gaps are much smaller in China. Consequently, as shown in Fig. 6.7, China will remain the world leader in terms of actual workers for several more decades, until 2060, despite having a lower working-age population from 2030. Indeed, the number of workers in China will also be declining, from 840 M in 2015 to 629 M in 2060, but the gap in labour force size in 2015 (840 M vs 458 M) between both countries is much higher than the gap for the working-age population (1022 M vs 848 M). Without a change in labour force participation rates, much more time is thus required for India to reach the level of China in terms of number of workers. This shows again the high stakes of including labour force participation as source of heterogeneity in population projections.

6.8 Overview of Results

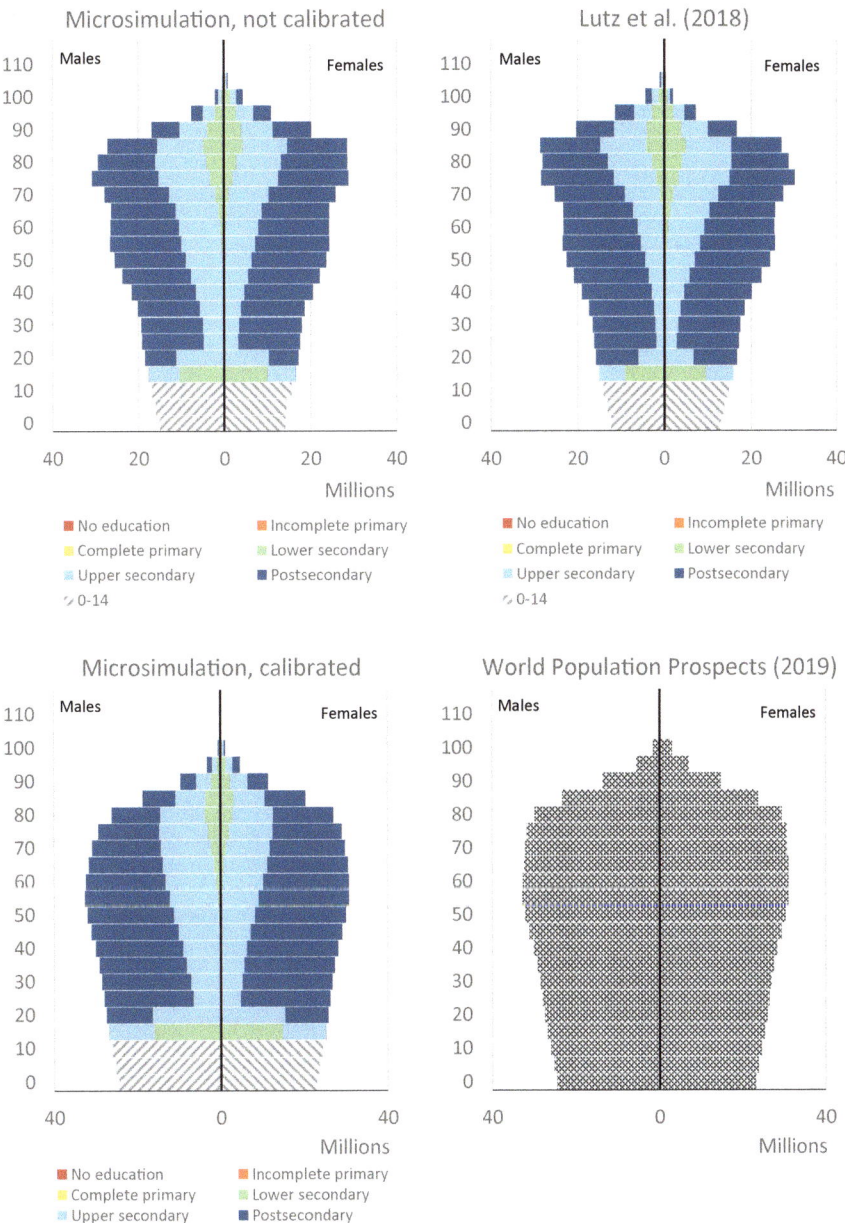

Fig. 6.6 Comparison of the projected age pyramid in 2100 by education in China from multistate models and from microsimulation

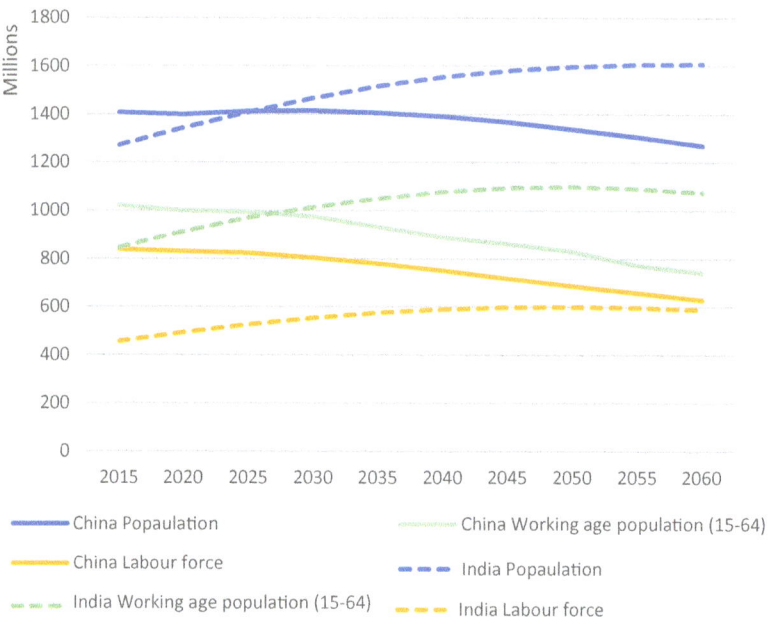

Fig. 6.7 Projected total population size, working-age population (15–64) size, and labour force size, India and China, 2015–2060

References

Basten, S., Sobotka, T., & Zeman, K. (2014). Future fertility in low fertility countries. In: W. Lutz, W. P. Butz, S. KC (Eds.), *World population and human capital in the 21st century* (pp. 39–146). Oxford: Oxford University Press.

KC, S., Wurzer, M., Speringer, M., & Lutz, W. (2018). Future population and human capital in heterogeneous India. *Proceedings of the National Academy of Sciences of the United States of America, 115*, 8328. https://doi.org/10.1073/pnas.1722359115

Lutz, W., Goujon, A., KC S., et al. (Eds.). (2018). *Demographic and human capital scenarios for the 21st century*. Luxembourg: Publications Office of the European Union.

UN. (2017). *World population prospects: The 2017 revision, key findings and advance tables*. New York: United Nations Population Division, Department of Economic and Social Affairs.

United Nations. (2019). *World population prospects: The 2019 revision*. New York, NY: Department of Economic and Social Affairs, Population Division.

Open Access This chapter is licensed under the terms of the Creative Commons Attribution 4.0 International License (http://creativecommons.org/licenses/by/4.0/), which permits use, sharing, adaptation, distribution and reproduction in any medium or format, as long as you give appropriate credit to the original author(s) and the source, provide a link to the Creative Commons license and indicate if changes were made.

The images or other third party material in this chapter are included in the chapter's Creative Commons license, unless indicated otherwise in a credit line to the material. If material is not included in the chapter's Creative Commons license and your intended use is not permitted by statutory regulation or exceeds the permitted use, you will need to obtain permission directly from the copyright holder.

Chapter 7
Conclusion

In this book, we have shown how to build a microsimulation model in the SAS language. Chap. 3 showed how to replicate a multistate model; Chap. 4 added two new dimensions; Chap. 5 offered examples of alternative scenarios and Chap. 6 demonstrated how to adapt the model for other uses.

The codes we proposed are adapted to specific contexts, but microsimulation models have the advantage of being very flexible. Beginning with the framework we presented, only minor changes would be required to adapt the codes to other uses and include more variables. Conditional on the availability of data, sociocultural variables such religion or language could be added, based on the modelling of the internal mobility module (Chap. 3). We could then use these variables to modulate fertility rates by applying relative risks or other types of parameters.

Alternatively, we could completely change the modelling of fertility by using logit regression parameters (see Potančoková and Marois (2020) for an example). In that case, we would merge parameters to the population file in the same way we did for the labour force participation and sector of activity modules, and then from those parameters, calculate each individual's probability within the model.

We could also change the modelling of education. Rather than applying transition rates from the age of 15, we could decide at birth the highest level of education an individual will reach during his or her lifetime, and then assign ages for graduations (see Marois et al. (2019) for an example of this modelling). This would allow us to take into account the education of the mother as a predictor of educational attainment with regression parameters.

Our labour force participation module assumes that the probability of being a worker is independent of past status. This was a constraint of data availability and not a constraint of the microsimulation method. Indeed, we model this module this way because our data source doesn't allow for calculating entry and exit rates. If those data existed, we might decide to model the event as the probability of leaving or entering the labour force. Again, this would only require changes in the parameter files and minor changes in the code of the equation (depending on the statistical model used).

References

Marois, G., Sabourin, P., & Bélanger, A. (2019). Forecasting human capital of EU member countries accounting for sociocultural determinants. *Journal of Demographic Economics, 85*, 231–269. https://doi.org/10.1017/dem.2019.4

Potančoková, M., & Marois, G. (2020). Projecting the future births in the EU28 with fertility differentials reflecting women's educational and migrant characteristics. Vienna Yearbook of Population Research.

Open Access This chapter is licensed under the terms of the Creative Commons Attribution 4.0 International License (http://creativecommons.org/licenses/by/4.0/), which permits use, sharing, adaptation, distribution and reproduction in any medium or format, as long as you give appropriate credit to the original author(s) and the source, provide a link to the Creative Commons license and indicate if changes were made.

The images or other third party material in this chapter are included in the chapter's Creative Commons license, unless indicated otherwise in a credit line to the material. If material is not included in the chapter's Creative Commons license and your intended use is not permitted by statutory regulation or exceeds the permitted use, you will need to obtain permission directly from the copyright holder.

GPSR Compliance

The European Union's (EU) General Product Safety Regulation (GPSR) is a set of rules that requires consumer products to be safe and our obligations to ensure this.

If you have any concerns about our products, you can contact us on

ProductSafety@springernature.com

In case Publisher is established outside the EU, the EU authorized representative is:

Springer Nature Customer Service Center GmbH
Europaplatz 3
69115 Heidelberg, Germany

www.ingramcontent.com/pod-product-compliance
Ingram Content Group UK Ltd.
Pitfield, Milton Keynes, MK11 3LW, UK
UKHW020241040925
462575UK00004B/185